the joy of
home distilling

home distilling

**The Ultimate Guide to Making Your Own Vodka, Whiskey,
Rum, Brandy, Moonshine, and More**

Rick Morris

Illustrations by Ericka Cummings

Skyhorse Publishing

Skyhorse Publishing books may be purchased in bulk at special
discounts for sales promotion, corporate gifts, fund-raising,
or educational purposes. Special editions can also be created to
specifications. For details, contact the Special Sales Department,
Skyhorse Publishing, 307 West 36th Street, 11th Floor, New York,
NY 10018 or info@skyhorsepublishing.com.

Skyhorse® and Skyhorse Publishing® are registered trademarks
of Skyhorse Publishing, Inc.®, a Delaware corporation.

Visit our website at www.skyhorsepublishing.com.
15

Library of Congress Cataloging-in-Publication Data is available
on file.

Cover design by LeAnna Weller Smith

Print ISBN: 978-1-62914-586-0
Ebook ISBN: 978-1-63220-011-2

Printed in China

CONTENTS

PART ②

DISTILL AT HOME

PART ③
RESOURCES

Dedication

The *Joy of Home Distilling* is dedicated to all those wiser than I, who took the time to teach me along my journey, and to all of those who may in turn learn from this book so that they may continue to pass this knowledge on to others.

I especially wish to thank my wife, Dawn, for her never-ending support and willingness to follow me down every path that I take, regardless of where it leads. Without her support, this book would not have been possible.

Introduction

What is distillation?

THE COMMON MISCONCEPTION about distilling is that it actually creates something. Many people who do not fully understand the process believe that when you distill a liquid, a new product is created in the process. This is not at all the case. By definition, distillation is simply a means of purifying a liquid by boiling the liquid and then condensing the vapors. Therefore, if the product that you wish to collect is not present in the liquid that you are going to distill, you will not be successful in your endeavor. This is true regardless of what you wish to distill, be it water, vinegar, fuel, perfume, or alcohol. The purpose of distilling is to separate the vapors to collect only the part or parts that you want. So, in reality, distillation is nothing more than a method of purification by boiling a liquid to separate the pieces that it is made up of, collecting those that you want, and discarding the remainder. This is possible because the individual compounds boil at different temperatures, and therefore we can be rather precise in what we are collecting.

Because it is so effective, distillation is used to produce many products, including water, fuel, vinegar, perfume, essential oils, pharmaceuticals, and, of course, alcohol. Naturally, one's mind seems to immediately jump to alcohol when we mention distillation.

Tell someone that you have a still, and you will often invoke a response confirming this belief. It is truly magical how a person's mind immediately assumes that you mean *alcohol distillation* when you say the word "still." Virtually never do you hear in response, "Oh, you distill water?" or the myriad of other distilled products that you could have been referring to. No, a person immediately envisions an old copper still back in the woods, with an aged man (complete with gray beard and denim overalls) standing beside a copper coil while clear liquor drips into a gallon jug. Yes, this still goes on back in the hills, but it is not what you were referring to. You were referring to far more refined equipment and the hobby that is akin to home beer- and winemaking, not a for-profit illegal enterprise. For our purposes, we will also focus on the distillation of alcohol and, more specifically, small production, or "hobby distilling."

Serious home distilling hobbyists may eventually gather the equipment and know-how necessary to build a small commercial system, such as this, to make their distillations.

So, now you know the basics of what distillation is and that you need alcohol present in the liquid that you intend to distill if you expect to collect any of it as a result of the process. But how do you create that alcohol in the first place? Alcohol is created through a process called fermentation, which is the same process used for making beer and wine. However, in the case of beer or wine, it is not put through the additional step of distillation. After the fermentation of wine or beer, it is generally cleared (to remove all yeast and other particles floating in the liquid), possibly aged, and then bottled. In the case of spirits such as vodka, rum, or whiskey, that fermented liquid, or "wash," as it is commonly called, is distilled. But if fermentation is how alcohol is created, why do we bother to distill it at all? The fermentation process is only able to reach rather low alcohol percentages, which is suitable for beer and wine, but due to the limitations of yeast—the magical little creature that makes the alcohol for us—it is not possible to achieve more than around 18 percent alcohol by volume (the percentage of a liquid that is alcohol). This will simply not do for virtually any alcoholic beverage other than beer or wine. Therefore, to increase the percentage of alcohol, we need to separate the alcohol from the water and other components in the wash. This is most effectively done through distillation. So creating spirits is really a two-stage process—fermentation followed by distillation.

Is home distilling legal?

Next begs the question, is this legal? In most countries in the world it is legal to make wine and beer, however, it is not legal in many countries to distill alcohol for personal use. However, beyond that, the laws on home distilling vary greatly from country to country, and in some cases, even laws from individual states or provinces in a country may be at odds with a federal law regarding distillation. You may notice that I did not say "alcohol distilling." This is for good reason. The vast array of laws in different countries ranges from it being illegal to so much as possess equipment capable of distilling alcohol (which would be very difficult to enforce, unless you make stock pots and mixing bowls illegal, but more on that later) to being entirely legal to distill alcohol at home for personal use. Some countries may not even necessarily disallow hobby alcohol distillation, but simply have no law that covers it. Obviously, we cannot even begin to offer a list that would cover every country in the world, and if we

A proper home distilling set up.
Photo courtesy Philip Shaner

tried, the list would likely be out of date as quickly as a new computer, as laws can and do change. I will, however, cover a few of the major countries where hobby alcohol distillation appears to be very much gaining interest, if not legal ground.

The best place to start is where it is most notably legal, namely New Zealand. Why New Zealand, of all places? Back in 1996, the law surrounding home distillation changed in New Zealand. This happened in stages, actually. It started in the 1980s, when the Labour Government decided to sell off many of the government departments to be run as private enterprises, converted to state-owned enterprises, or, for those where neither was a feasible option, the department would be run as a business with the intent of turning a profit. The Customs Department is an example of the latter. This created a quandary for the Customs Department, as they were tasked with checking on all licensed stills, even though many were not used for alcohol distillation, and therefore no revenue would be collected. This would create a large operational cost, with reduced revenue—hardly an optimal situation when they are expected to be turning a profit. In response to this concern, the government removed a section from the act that made ownership of an unlicensed still illegal. This still created an issue, however, as it was now legal to own a distiller, but not to distill alcohol without the appropriate license. Now that owning a still was legal, there was an explosion of stills being sold for home use, and while the Customs Department could require you to have a license and pay excise tax for the privilege of distilling alcohol at home, they found the very thought of the process to be potentially overwhelming and not profitable, so they largely ignored it. This is much the same stage that many countries, including the United States and Canada, are at today. Distillation of alcohol is illegal, but policing it would be an overwhelming and ultimately very costly task. When the liquor laws were changed again in 1996, the act was changed by adding the term spirits into the same section that covered the making of beer and wine, and legal home distillation of alcohol in New Zealand was born.

So, why only in New Zealand? Why not in other countries, such as the United States or Canada? The government will justify their stance by saying that the reason for making alcohol distillation illegal is for your safety. They suggest that homemade spirits are less safe than those produced commercially, despite the fact that, in many cases, a home distilled spirit contains fewer impurities than its commercial equivalent. In the book *Spirits Unlimited—A Complete Guide to Home Distilling* by Wheeler and Willmott, they show home distilled spirits actually to be considerably cleaner than commercial spirits:

"Home distilled spirit (untreated): methanol 0.0067 percent, ethanol 99.632 percent, fusils 0.361 percent

"Commercial vodka: methanol 0.013 percent, ethanol 99.507 percent, fusils 0.48 percent"

The government may also suggest that the act of distilling is dangerous, as the product is flammable, and if proper care is not taken it can result in injury or death. However, in our research of New Zealand, where home alcohol distillation is legal, we have been unable to find a single instance of injury, illness, death, or even damage to a structure to substantiate this suggestion. As there have been such issues in the United States and Canada, albeit few, that would tend to suggest that legalizing the hobby, which allows people to discuss it more freely and brings it out of the shadows, would actually make the hobby safer. Another claim may be concern over alcoholism and increased alcohol use. After all, it only stands to reason that when you make alcohol as freely accessible as home distillation does, alcohol consumption is bound to increase. Based on the World Health Organization's data, the 2003–2005 adult consumption of alcohol in liters of pure alcohol stood at 9.4L in the United States, compared with 9.8L in Canada and 9.6L in New Zealand, placing New Zealand squarely in the middle. Possibly an even more important figure is that for alcohol use disorders. According to the same data, the percentage of the populace with alcohol-related disorders is 3.7 percent in the United States (5.48 percent among males, 1.92 percent among females), 3.675 percent in Canada (5.43 percent among males, 1.92 percent among females), and only a combined 2.85 percent in New Zealand (3.5 percent among males, 2.2 percent among females). This would appear to be in direct contrast to conventional thinking, but instead it creates one more example of how allowing distilling of alcohol as a hobby does not cause the catastrophic events that most governments would have us believe.

So, with all of this evidence to the contrary, why would the government tell us that the legal stance on alcohol distillation is for our own protection? That is very simple—taxes. The government makes a tremendous amount of money by taxing alcohol. According to the World Health Organization's Global Health Observatory Data Repository, the excise tax from alcohol in the United States in 2009 stands at more than $9 billion! That is certainly a substantial tax to put at risk. Break that down over the 305 million people in the United States in 2009, and it equates to approximately $29.84 in excise tax for every American. Canadian figures are even more substantial on a per-capita basis, with over $5.3 billion in revenue for a population of approximately 33.5 million, for $158.21 per capita. And where does New Zealand sit in comparison? With home distillation of alcohol being legal, the government must see dramatically lower revenue from alcohol, right? Not so— roughly $591 million in excise tax over a population of approximately 4.4 million people gives them approximately $134.32 per person. Ah yes, but what would it have been if they had not legalized home alcohol distillation? It surely would have been much higher. To know this, we must look back to the figures just prior to legalization in 1996. So, in 1995, here were the numbers:

Excise tax from alcohol in 1995: $378.34 million
Population: 4.3 million
Excise tax per capita: $87.99

Wait a minute, this cannot be correct! Are we to believe that the excise tax from alcohol actually increased by more than 50 percent per capita since legalization of home distilling took effect? Yes, it appears, based on the data, that legalizing alcohol distillation not only had no substantial negative impact on revenues from alcohol, but it may have even played a role in increasing them. To further substantiate this, let's look at the 1995 figures for the United States:

Excise tax from alcohol in 1995: $7.52 billion
Population: 266 million
Excise tax per capita: $28.27

So, in the same time period that saw a growth in tax revenue on alcohol of more than 50 percent in New Zealand, the growth in the United States has been just over 5 percent. While this is certainly not meant to suggest that the legalization of home distilling of alcohol in New Zealand was be responsible for the substantial growth in alcohol based revenue, we can safely surmise that it has had no deleterious effect on those revenues. With this being the case, why would other countries, such as the United States and Canada, who supposedly have the greatest degree of personal freedom in the world, not follow suit? That remains a mystery, but undoubtedly it is simply a matter of educating our elected officials and making them realize that their concern over the potential lost revenue that legalizing home distilling would have is simply unfounded, and in fact, possibly at contrary to the actual results that legalization would bring. We must also remember that our representatives are not necessarily well informed on this particular subject and most likely have the same beliefs that the vast majority of people do, believing that the distillation process actually creates something dangerous. They need to be informed that what is created is done during the fermentation process, which is already legal in most places and that the distillation process actually removes many of the unwanted and potentially harmful components.

To that end, at the time of this writing, there is currently a legalization effort ongoing in the United States, headed by still producer Brewhaus America Inc. and a few enthusiastic participants from their discussion forum. Much time and effort has been put into the endeavor, and just as with the case in New Zealand, it will not happen overnight. Fortunately there are a few involved who will continue to press for legalization at a hobby level, and they will not be easily deterred. I expect hobbyists in other countries, who must continue to stay in the shadows with their hobby, to follow the lead that those involved in the legalization effort in the United States have forged.

PART 1

Understanding the Process

1. Yeast

IN THE BEGINNING there was yeast. Then came *hic* alcohol! Well, that may oversimplify things just a bit. The actual origins of fermentation go back roughly 5,000 years to ancient Egypt, when it is said that some grain was left outside in the rain accidentally (and ingeniously, I might add). Wild yeast on the grain resulted in fermentation, and the chain of events had some awfully interesting results. So, alcohol's roots are not exactly movie-worthy, but the progression to today's refined alcohol—be it beer, wine, mead, whiskey, rum, vodka, etc.—are much more interesting. But, you are not here to learn about ancient Egypt, are you? So, let's get to it!

Yeast is properly defined as a fungus, and it is a single-celled organism that, for our purposes, consumes sugar in an aqueous solution and converts it into alcohol. It is somewhat more complex than this, which I shall explain shortly, but the important fact here is that

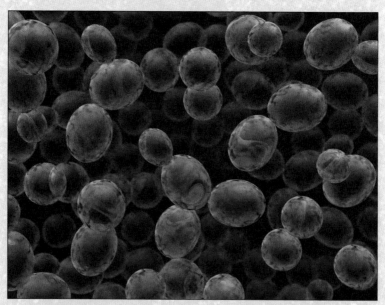

Yeast under a microscope.

sugar + water + yeast = alcohol. It is important to note that there are many different types of alcohol, but the one that we are generally referring to when we use the term alcohol is actually ethanol. Methanol is another alcohol that is often formed in small amounts during fermentation, and for our purposes, it is not desirable. In fact, we strive to make as much ethanol and as little of other alcohols as possible. Knowing this basic fact, we can now look at the life cycle of the yeast cell and how to get what we want from it.

Nutrition

While yeast is a simple organism, it still has rather complex nutritional requirements if it is going to perform to the best of its abilities. Just like you and I require nutrition to go about our daily tasks, yeast does too. Yes, yeast has far simpler nutritional requirements than we do, but it still requires adequate nutrition to do its job. If you add yeast to a simple sugar and water solution, you can sit back, relax, and watch the yeast do nothing. It is really not all that exciting to watch. Add the proper nutrients, vitamins, and minerals to that same mixture, however, and you will see the yeast come to life and happily consume all of the sugar in the solution, replacing it with alcohol.

Adequate nutrition is generally achieved in one of two ways: either by adding the individual nutrients, minerals, and vitamins to a sugar water solution or by using nutrient-rich ingredients, such as grains or fruit. Both options have advantages and disadvantages. While adding all of the necessary nutritional pieces to the solution will allow you to ferment a simple sugar and water solution—the simplest wash to create—unless you have both a chemistry degree and access to all of the individual ingredients, it is not a simple task. Well, that is not entirely true, but it certainly wasn't just a few years ago. Nowadays you can purchase "turbo yeast," which is a mixture of highly alcohol-tolerant yeast *plus* all of the nutrients that the yeast needs. This may sound like a great solution, but it does not come without its drawbacks, which will be discussed later.

The second option is to use ingredients like grain, such as those used in the brewing industry. These grains will provide the nutrition that our little yeast friends need to do their jobs, as well as potentially providing sugar for the yeast to consume and turn into alcohol for us. I say potentially providing sugar because in grains, the sugars come in the form of starches, which are essentially long-chained sugars, and they must first be broken down into shorter-chained sugars to be fully utilized by the yeast during the fermentation process. Another option for nutrient-rich ingredients is fruit, although many types of fruit are lacking in some of the nutrients that the yeast requires. In the case of fruit, most of the micronutrients are provided, so you can add normal winemaking complex nutrients (commonly sold as Yeast Energizer) or select one of the yeast mixtures that has been developed specifically for this type of fermentation.

With adequate nutrition having been considered, there is another important factor that we need to consider: oxygen. Yeast will convert the sugar into alcohol, but only if it is starved of oxygen. This is known as anaerobic fermentation. In the presence of oxygen, yeast is very inefficient at fermentation. However, yeast does require oxygen at the onset of fermentation. In the presence of oxygen, yeast will bud and reproduce, making more yeast cells. This is actually a very useful piece of information, as it allows you to control what the yeast is going to do once you combine it with your nutrient-rich sugar solution. If you do not pitch (toss in) enough yeast to do the job, then fermentation will be very sluggish, as there are simply not enough yeast cells to consume the sugar very quickly. The yeast needs more friends and family to help out.

By stirring the mixture vigorously, we can usually drive enough oxygen into the liquid to give the yeast the opportunity to use a small amount of that sugar to multiply. During this part of the process, the yeast will consume the oxygen and take up many of the nutrients in the solution while it multiplies, which it does through a process called budding. Once the oxygen is exhausted, the yeast will get to work converting your sugar into alcohol. The time during which the yeast is multiplying is known as a *lag phase*. You will generally see little visible action during this time aside, from a slight head of yeast building on the top of your wash, and it can range from less than an hour to as much as a day, but is usually less than 12 hours. In fact, if you continue to drive oxygen into your mixture for the entire process, you can make yourself a nice big bucket of yeast with very little alcohol production. But obviously we don't want that.

Stress on the Yeast

With that said, it does get a little bit more complex. Different strains of yeast have slightly different nutritional requirements. Without proper nutrition, that is, the correct balance of the different minerals, nutrients, and vitamins, the yeast will not perform to the best of its ability. Lack of proper nutrition will cause stress on the yeast. Stressed yeast will produce by-products that result in not only a foul-smelling and foul-tasting product, but for every bit of sugar that the yeast converts into by-products, there is less sugar being converted into alcohol. Therefore it is in our own best interest to go the extra mile to keep our little yeast friends happy, and they will make us happier in return.

Lack of nutrition is only one potential stress on your yeast. You will also always want to maintain a watchful eye over your fermentation temperature to ensure that it remains within the "happy zone" for your particular yeast. The optimal temperature range varies by yeast strain and type, so there is no one-size-fits-all range to recommend. Most yeast packages will specify the optimal temperature range both for pitching (which is often higher than the optimal temperature range to maintain during fermentation) and the recommended temperature range for fermentation. The temperature range listed on the yeast package is very important. Fermenting at the lower end of the temperature range will usually result in slower fermentation, and falling below the minimum recommended temperature will see extremely slow fermentation or even result in fermentation ceasing altogether. As you near the top end of the temperature range, your fermentation speed will increase. However, the elevated temperature can also stress out our little yeast friends, and in return for your neglect, they will produce increased byproducts in place of a small amount of alcohol. Always remember that if you do not take care of your yeast, they will get revenge.

Yet another stress on the yeast that is often overlooked is the optimal maximum alcohol tolerance of the yeast, which can be further divided into two sections—before and after. In the before zone, we have to consider the stress created as you increase the sugar content in your mixture. With a greater concentration of sugar, you create greater stress on the yeast cells. It is actually possible to increase the sugar content to the point where the yeast simply cannot ferment it. Even as you near this maximum sugar concentration you will create an ever-increasing stress on the yeast. This stress will increase the production of by-products during fermentation. The "after" stress is the percentage of alcohol that you are requesting of the yeast. Each strain of yeast has a limit on the percentage of alcohol that it can survive in. Yeast does not start out with this tolerance, but rather builds it as the alcohol content in the wash rises. Therefore you cannot put yeast with a tolerance to 18 percent alcohol into a mixture that already contains 15 percent alcohol and expect it to perform. This sudden immersion into the alcoholic mixture will kill the yeast. When we refer to yeast's alcohol tolerance, we are actually referring to the percentage of alcohol that it can build its tolerance to. Sound confusing? It is actually very simple. As yeast converts more and more sugar into alcohol, and the percentage alcohol in the wash rises, so does the yeast's tolerance to alcohol. It will hit a certain point, however, where the poor little yeast can take no more and will cough, sputter, and die. You can actually hear it begging for its life (well, not really, but if you have indulged a bit too much, you may at least hear the coughing and sputtering). I guess you could say that yeast is almost like a guppy; it will eat and eat until it literally dies of its own overindulgence. I have seen this personally and can assure that you that it is not a pretty sight. So it is important to know the maximum alcohol tolerance of the particular yeast strain you are using and to stay a little bit below this to avoid added stress.

Combined stress. So you know the optimal temperature range of the yeast strain and its alcohol tolerance. What if you near the limits on just one of those? Then the yeast's tolerance for the other is reduced. For example, if you get very near the top end of the yeast's temperature limit, it will not be able to squeeze out quite as much alcohol. The combined stress will be too much, and it will die out before achieving its normal maximum alcohol potential. So it is best to avoid pushing the extremes of the yeast without knowing exactly what you are doing and just what the repercussions will be.

Yeast Storage

A very important factor in how viable your yeast will be is the storage conditions of the yeast. Although dried yeast is "sleeping" and far less vulnerable to poor storage conditions than hydrated yeast, it is still susceptible to a variety of factors. Because most yeast you purchase for fermentation will be either vacuum-packed or nitrogen-flushed (where the package is flushed with nitrogen to remove the oxygen), you will not generally have to be concerned with spoilage due to air having access to your yeast. Air is of concern for two reasons. First is oxygen. Even in dry form, yeast is susceptible to harm from oxygen. Oxygen will greatly reduce the shelf life of the yeast by accelerating the loss of viable yeast cells. Therefore, when you pitch your yeast into the wash, you will actually be using fewer live yeast cells, resulting in a longer lag phase and fewer active cells to convert the sugar into alcohol. This results in a slower fermentation. In addition, as the yeast cells can only do so much work before they settle to the bottom of the vessel and go dormant or die, under-pitching can result in an incomplete fermentation. Air is also of concern because it carries bacteria and wild yeast, which would then be added to your wash when you pitch your yeast. These can cause spoilage, bad flavors, and a multitude of other fermentation issues. For these reasons it is highly advised to avoid purchasing "bulk" format yeast, unless you will be using it all within a very short time frame. I especially discourage purchasing bulk format yeast that has been repacked without proper equipment. With the increased interest in hobby distillation, some suppliers have taken to packaging bulk yeast for resale to reduce cost and increase profit. Generally, if it is not vacuum-packed or packed in foil pouches with wide seals, then it has most likely been repacked by hand by a reseller without proper equipment. In such cases the yeast has already begun to lose viability long before you ever purchase it. If you have purchased bulk yeast, then it is best to store the opened package by rolling it tightly to remove as much air as possible and keeping it in the refrigerator to slow the effects of air on the yeast.

Another important storage factor is the temperature that the yeast is stored at. While properly packaged yeast can be stored for extended periods at room temperature, or indeed even at a somewhat elevated temperature, storing at a cooler temperature will help extend the life of the yeast cells. Keep in mind that the expiration date or "best before" date on the package is taking into account standard storage conditions. That is, the manufacturer assumes storage at or below normal room temperature. If your yeast is stored at a higher temperature, then it will deteriorate more quickly and may not have any viable cells remaining even before the date printed on the package. Similarly, storing your yeast at a lower temperature will help extend the life of the yeast, meaning that it may remain viable well beyond the expiration date on the package. It is also recommended to try to maintain a consistent temperature when storing your yeast, as temperature fluctuations can affect its viability. Storing your yeast in a refrigerator is an excellent option, however, extra planning must be undertaken before you can use your yeast if it has been stored this way. The thermal shock of taking your cold yeast and pitching it directly into a warm wash will almost always kill the yeast. It is not at all uncommon for a person to mix their wash, take the yeast from the refrigerator to pitch into the wash, and end up with no fermentation. To avoid this pitfall, always take your yeast from the fridge several hours before you plan to use it to allow it to slowly come to room temperature.

Effects of Yeast on Flavor

It hard to believe, but this little package of yeast actually has a rather significant impact on the flavor and aroma of your finished product. As part of the fermentation process—or actually, more correctly, the stage before active fermentation begins—yeast will produce flavor and aroma compounds. This is done while the yeast is taking up oxygen and some of the nutrients in the wash and as it multiplies and builds its colony. Although the amount of yeast pitched appears to be very small given the volume of liquid that you are inoculating, it is one of the greatest contributors of flavor and aroma, with only the primary ingredients (type of fruit, grain, etc.) having a greater impact on the characteristics of the finished product. Because the yeast that you select has such a great impact on the flavor and aroma of your finished product, it is important to select the most appropriate yeast style for the product that you wish to make. An entire book could be dedicated to listing all of the different characteristics between individual strains, such as different strands of whiskey yeast. That is best left for commercial distilleries who are trying to create special nuances in their products to make them stand apart from that of their competitors. For our purposes, I will only discuss the major yeast groups and not the different strains of yeast within each of those groups.

Types of Yeast

While virtually all types of yeast will consume sugar and create alcohol, given proper nutrition and the right set of conditions, there are several yeast styles available commercially that have been optimized for fermentation. The most commonly used yeast types for brewing, winemaking, and distilling are *Saccharomyces cerevisiae* and *Saccharomyces bayanus*. Even within these two groups fall several different strains, each with its own characteristics and flavor-producing profile. I will not go into detail about the differences between individual yeast strands, however, it is important to discuss how the different yeast choices will affect your fermentation and, ultimately, your finished product.

Neutral Fermenting Yeasts

As the name implies, this group of yeasts will generally have the smallest contribution to flavor and aroma. Their purpose is to produce a fermented wash with as little flavor as possible and are most suited for vodka or other neutral spirits that will then be flavored, either with the addition of essence or by infusion. Neutral fermenting yeasts are also the most commonly used type of yeast in fuel alcohol production, as they often have the highest alcohol tolerance.

Fruit Yeasts

Although you are not reading this book to learn how to make wine, you are ultimately making just that when you intend to produce brandy, schnapps, or any other fruit-based spirit. Quite simply, what you have made prior to the distillation of a fruit-based fermentation is wine. If you wanted to, you could stop after fermentation, bottle the undistilled product, and have a good bottle of wine. At least I hope that it is good wine. If it isn't, then it will not produce a good distilled spirit. Remember, distillation does not *make* anything. So if you do not have good flavor to start with, then you might as well go straight to a neutral spirit distillation, as you will be sorely disappointed with the flavor of your spirit otherwise.

So, with that said, wine yeast is intended for use with fruit and should enhance the flavor and aroma of the fruit that you are using. Now, in wine production, where your intent is **not** to distill the product but instead to bottle the product as wine, there are numerous different strains within the wine yeast category, each offering different nuances and flavor notes, and often even recommendations of specific grape species that they best complement. For our purposes, however, it is sufficient to consider all wine and fruit yeasts as a single group.

In short, fruit yeasts are intended to enhance and bring out as much fruit character as possible, and to that end the yeast will produce fruity esters and flavor compounds.

Whiskey Yeast

Basically, whiskey yeast is simply a high alcohol tolerant type of beer yeast. Whiskey is, in slightly simplified terms, distilled unhopped beer. Of course, most whiskey is aged in or with oak or some other type of wood, but the basics are the same—it is made from a grain mash or wash comprised of malt extract. This being the case, the yeasts used to make whiskey are very similar to those used for making beer, but generally with higher tolerance to alcohol. However, the basic flavor and aroma profiles produced by the yeast will be very similar to those from beer yeast. As with wine yeast, there are many different styles of beer yeast, however, most beer yeasts have a lower tolerance to alcohol than whiskey yeast.

Rum Yeast

Not really a yeast group, the yeasts used to produce rum are again selected based on the type of substrate that they are best at fermenting and the flavor profile that they produce. As rum is a spirit distilled from molasses, it is best to use a yeast strain that is proficient with fermenting molasses, while maximizing flavor carryover into the fermented wash.

Baker's Yeast

Baking yeast is not intended for the production of beverage-grade alcohol. However, it is used by some as a cost-saving mechanism. While it will ferment your wash and produce alcohol, as will any yeast (it is yeast's purpose in life, after all), the alcohol tolerance and especially its flavor production profile are not well suited to distilled spirit production.

Turbo Yeast

While this is not actually a type of yeast, with the immense popularity and substantial difference in format versus standard yeast, it really deserves independent discussion. Turbo yeast, also known as super yeast, has grown to include virtually all yeast and nutrient mixes, but in real terms, turbo yeast is a much larger than normal volume of yeast combined with a complex mixture of nutrients, minerals, and vitamins such that it will provide an extremely fast and complete fermentation. The idea behind the development of turbo yeast was originally to provide a fast fermentation, saving time for the commercial and hobby distiller. You can imagine that in a commercial operation, this savings of time can result in increased profit, as more product can be produced without having to increase space or the number of fermenters being used in the operation. At the hobby level, it is simply a matter of convenience. The other thing that turbo yeast was developed to do was provide all of the nutrition that the yeast needs so that a wash completely devoid of nutrition for the yeast, such as simple sugar water, could be fermented. The advantages to such a leap forward in fermentation virtually go without saying.

Now you know the pros of using turbo yeast: it will provide you with a quick and complete fermentation, even when your wash is lacking in nutrition. So why wouldn't everyone use turbo yeast for every wash? Turbo yeast is not without its disadvantages, and when coupled with most people's lack of understanding of the process, it is easy to find someone with a negative feeling toward turbo yeast. First and foremost is cost. Although hobby distilling is far less about cost savings than home brewing or home winemaking, that does not mean that people are not cost-conscious. While you can easily find brewer's or winemaker's yeast for a dollar or less, turbo yeasts generally cost upward of $3 to $5, and some places as much as $10. Having learned all about the importance of nutrition and how a lack of nutrition impacts your fermentation, though, you are not about to risk your entire batch for just a couple of dollars, right? Well, there is more, so maybe wait on that decision just a little longer.

Another reason that some people have negative feelings toward turbo yeast is because they do not understand exactly why yeast produces by-products, which present themselves as "off" flavors and aromas. Sulfur is a perfect example and certainly the most noticeable of the by-products formed during fermentation. In most cases, a person using turbo yeast is doing so with a simple sugar wash, therefore there are no outside flavor and aroma profiles to help mask the by-products produced. With a grain wash, fruit wash, molasses wash, etc., there is sufficient flavor and aroma to mask most of the by-products produced during fermentation. As a result, some people think that these natural yeast by-products are caused by using turbo yeast. Basically, you can smell and taste them (by tasting the wash during or after fermentation) much more easily in a sugar wash because there is nothing else to taste. Try the same thing with a fruit-based wash or molasses wash, and many of these by-products, while present, will be practically unnoticeable.

Another issue is that, in many cases, people will push the limits of a turbo yeast far more than a non-turbo yeast. What I mean is that they will aim for a higher alcohol content when using turbo yeast. This is stressor number one. And with a non-turbo yeast, the fermentation is slower, thus the wash generally stays at a lower temperature. Stressor number two: as you know by now, pushing the limits of the yeast will increase the stress on it, and when you increase the stress level on the yeast, it will increase the production of by-products. With a good-quality turbo yeast, if you do not cause undue stress (i.e., keep the temperature and specific gravity from the upper range for the yeast), then you will get a very clean, complete, and rapid fermentation.

Now, with all of this said, you will often get slightly more off flavors with a traditional turbo yeast because of the use of urea as a major component. Urea is also a concern, as it can increase the production of ethyl carbamate, which is believed to be a carcinogen. While some ethyl carbamate will be produced in almost any fermentation, a new line of urea-free turbo yeasts is becoming more mainstream, resulting in a slightly cleaner-tasting finished product that should have reduced levels of ethyl carbamate.

Another consideration when opting for a turbo yeast is that unused nutrients will remain in the wash at the end of fermentation. While they can be removed during distillation, they certainly can contribute to an unpleasant smell and taste in the fermented wash, and they are also costing you money needlessly. All of the ingredients in your package of turbo yeast add to the cost, so if you are leaving nutrients unused, you are simply throwing money away.

There is one final thing to remember if you are using turbo yeast. While many home brewers and winemakers will rehydrate the yeast in a small amount of water prior to pitching it into the wash, doing this with a turbo yeast is not only unnecessary, but must actually be avoided. While all of the nutrients in the turbo yeast package are necessary for the yeast to perform well, they are toxic to the yeast in high concentrations. This means that the best intentions of an experienced winemaker or brewer, intending to keep their little yeast friends happy by rehydrating, as they are so used to doing, will actually kill the yeast. This leads to frustration and can even lead to ruined batches because a wild yeast or bacteria could get hold of your wash. The best advice is always to follow the instructions on your yeast package, and if it does not recommend rehydrating your yeast prior to pitching, then don't.

Finally, remember this whole list of yeast styles and how they affect flavor and aroma. Given that turbo yeast was primarily developed to work with sugar wash fermentation, they generally use a neutral fermenting yeast style. This makes a standard turbo yeast less than optimal for fermenting other washes, such as fruit or grain. To combat this, there are now "specialty turbo yeasts." These yeasts use only the nutrients needed to complete the fermentation for their specific purpose, saving you money and helping avoid off flavors from residual unused nutrients. Some also use specific yeast strains for their touted purpose, meaning that a product sold for whiskey fermentation may use a whiskey yeast strain or a fruit yeast strain for a turbo yeast meant for fruit fermentation. Unfortunately, some brands may be less reputable and simply use the lowest cost strain regardless of the use, so this is a case where I definitely advise sticking to one of the few recognized brands and avoiding privately labeled "house brands."

Dried Active Distiller's Yeast (DADY)

This is a general, "all-purpose" style of highly alcohol-tolerant yeast that is commonly sold at homebrew supply stores, often to unsuspecting customers who are trying to save a few dollars over purchasing turbo yeast. Given its name—"distiller's yeast"—many people believe that it is a bulk turbo yeast, and unfortunately many homebrew stores that sell this product are unable to assist when you pitch it into your wash and nothing happens. Just remember that this yeast is precisely what it says it is. It is yeast and nothing more. Now, that is not to say that it does not have its place. If your wash is providing sufficient nutrition for the yeast, and you are able to use all of the yeast in a reasonably short amount of time, then it can definitely be a very cost-effective option. Usually sold in 1.1-pound (500g) bags, it is substantially lower in cost per use than turbo yeast. However, if your wash does not provide adequate nutrition for the yeast, then you are back to square one. To counteract this issue, there is a product available known as distiller's nutrients, which, unlike the yeast nutrients or yeast energizer sold by most homebrew supply stores, is basically a complete turbo yeast nutrient mix. Essentially, it is turbo yeast without the yeast.

2. Fermentation

JESUS TURNED WATER into wine. The rest of us have to use fermentation.

As you know by now, the first step of the distillation process is fermentation. This process is the same whether you are fermenting to make beer, wine, or distilled spirits. In many cases the recipe is even very similar or, in some cases, identical to that used to make beer or wine. For example, to make brandy, you will ferment a grape mash just as you would to make grape wine and then distill the finished wine into brandy. Whiskey is basically a fermented and distilled unhopped beer, and rum is a fermented and distilled wash made from molasses. Yes, more generally goes into these different spirits after the distillation process has been completed, such as aging in wood barrels, but you get the basic idea.

The fermentation process can actually be very involved and complex, so it is important to fully understand what is going on during fermentation, things to watch for, how to avoid common mistakes that can taint or ruin a batch, and how to get back on track if you experience any difficulties. To that end, let's start back with yeast and exactly what it is doing throughout the fermentation process.

Yeast Life Cycle

Many people step into brewing and distillation with a misunderstanding of what really takes place during fermentation. Beginning brewers who are more interested in the finished product than understanding the process will just take a malt extract beer kit, dissolve it in water, pitch the yeast, and expect the product to turn out. Often it does. Sometimes it does not, and in most cases a ruined batch could have been easily avoided with some basic knowledge of what is actually taking place, as this will not only arm them with the knowledge needed to ensure that they do things correctly from the start, but also the ability to recognize and correct an issue before it ruins their product. They do not even realize that this tiny packet of yeast they pitch into the fermenter does more than swell up and disperse itself when it is introduced to the mash, but it will go through several stages, from multiplying and increasing the yeast cells in the wash to the actual conversion of sugar into alcohol. The basic stages in the yeast's life cycle are aerobic respiration (or lag phase), fermentation, and sedimentation. However, before you even mix your wash, it is imperative that you clean and sanitize your fermentation equipment thoroughly to avoid ruining your wash with bacteria, wild yeast, or molds that are just as interested in your yummy mixture as your yeast is. Because sanitation is not part of the life cycle of the yeast, it will be discussed later.

Aerobic Respiration

Commonly known as the lag phase, this is what takes place when you first pitch your yeast into the wash. With a dried yeast, which is what you will be using in most cases, it will first quickly rehydrate (take up liquid) and then enter the lag phase. This is when yeast rapidly absorbs oxygen and takes up minerals and nitrogen in the wash. Oxygen is extremely important at this stage, as the yeast will utilize it in reproduction and the construction of cell walls. The yeast also derives energy from the available oxygen and sugar, which it will need to carry it through the entire fermentation process. In addition to reproduction, yeast will consume sugar and produce water, carbon dioxide, and some flavor and aroma compounds during aerobic respiration. However, no alcohol is produced during this stage. At this point you will notice a layer of foam, known as krausen, build on the top of your wash. How large the krausen is will depend on your strain of yeast and the composition of your wash. It does not necessarily directly correlate to the ultimate speed of fermentation. The lag phase will last from two or three hours and up to several hours. Immediately following the lag phase is . . .

Fermentation

Finally, the moment you have been waiting for! Your little yeast buddies are turning your big bucket of sugar, fruit, grain, or whatever into that delicious elixir that you have been working so hard for. This stage can be very interesting for the new brewer, as the activities taking place can be seen far more than those in the lag phase. The krausen formed during the lag phase will "fall" into the wash, and your wash will become noticeably lighter in color due to the growing number of yeast cells in suspension. Reproduction will continue to take place until the yeast has reached its optimal concentration of around 50 million cells per milliliter of wash. Yes, you read that correctly, and now you also know why your once-clear wash will become extremely cloudy. At the same time, the yeast is rapidly consuming sugar and converting it into carbon dioxide and . . . alcohol. Yes, alcohol. At last, we are getting somewhere! At this stage, you will see and smell the activity. If you use a sealed fermenter with an airlock, you will see the bubbles racing through it. If you look at the top of the wash, it will be very active, with the carbon dioxide that is being produced making it look

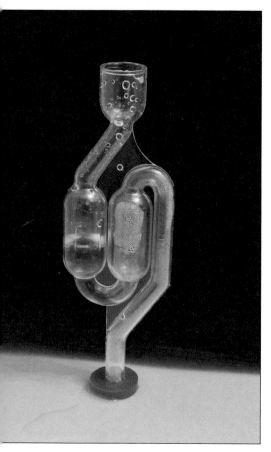

like a big container of soda pop, and you'll even hear the fizzle as the bubbles break. Esters that are produced by the yeast, along with a host of other by-products, will be carried out by the carbon dioxide, so you may notice a cidery or yeasty aroma during this stage. Fermentation is an anaerobic process (i.e., without oxygen), therefore oxygen is no longer a requirement of the yeast, and any oxygen remaining in the solution at this point will be removed by the carbon dioxide that is being produced. It is important to avoid the introduction of oxygen at this point, however, as it can have seriously negative effects on your final product. As the yeast cannot utilize oxygen introduced at this stage, it can potentially lead to oxidation, depending on what exactly you are fermenting, which can come across as a stale character in your finished product. Fermentation can take from a day or two for extremely rapid types of turbo yeast to a week or more for very high alcohol–style fermentations. Certain types of fermentation can take considerably longer than this, but those are generally special fermentations, such as when lagering beer or making mead. In most cases, fermentation of more than a week to ten days points to a potential problem. However, do not simply gauge fermentation by watching your airlock, as even once fermentation is complete you may see some activity through your airlock due to the carbon dioxide that was absorbed into the wash during fermentation slowly coming out of solution. It is always wise to check for completion of fermentation using a hydrometer.

Sedimentation

During the fermentation stage, yeast will consume sugar and slowly use up its energy stores from the lag phase. As its energy stores deplete and the food source (sugar) has been mostly consumed, it will begin to flocculate and settle to the bottom of the fermenter. The yeast is not dying, but simply going dormant. Depending on several factors, including the original nutrition in the wash, strain, and strength of the yeast and amount of stress encountered during the fermentation process, this can be at any time after about mid-fermentation. The speed of fermentation will decrease, and you may start to notice a layer of sediment building on the bottom of your fermenter. If you are concerned that fermentation has not finished, you can check for completion with a hydrometer. There are many factors that can lead to the yeast settling prematurely, in which case you may need to carefully stir the wash to rouse the yeast back into suspension. If you do this, then be sure to stir gently so as not to introduce oxygen into the wash. As fermentation completes, the yeast will continue to settle to the bottom of the fermentation vessel, leaving a clear liquid to siphon across into your kettle when you move on to distillation.

Hydrometers and test cylinders are essential tools for testing samples of your wash.

There are several factors that affect the speed at which the yeast will naturally fall to the bottom of the fermenter, including the strain of yeast being used, temperature of the liquid, and amount of dissolved gas in the wash. During the fermentation process, some of the carbon dioxide that is created gets absorbed into the liquid as microscopic bubbles. These bubbles can interfere with the yeast's ability to fall out of solution, so it is very helpful to de-gas the wash to aid the yeast in completing its journey to the bottom of your fermenter as quickly as possible. This can be done by agitating the wash several times and will work much like shaking a can of soda pop. The agitation helps release the dissolved gas, clearing the way for the yeast to fall out of solution unobstructed. And just as a can of soda will tend to lose its carbonation more quickly when it is warm than when it is cold, your wash will also release the dissolved carbon dioxide more quickly if it is warm. Agitating the wash can be as simple as removing the lid from your fermenter and stirring with a sanitized plastic brewing spoon or paddle. Wait 30 to 60 minutes and repeat this process. You will usually find that after repeating this process four or five times, you will see very little activity and you know that your wash is adequately de-gassed.

While de-gassing is best done with the liquid on the warmer side, clearing takes place more quickly when the wash is cool. This part of the process is just a waiting game, so if you are unable to decrease the wash temperature relatively easily, do not worry, as it will just add a couple of extra days to the process. You can also speed this process along using clearing agents, which will be discussed later.

So there you have it. You now know more about yeast than you probably ever cared to know. But you plan to make superior spirits, right? You are going to rival the finest commercial products in the store and knock those big guys from their perch! If you intend to produce such fine products, you need to know what is taking place, and now you have a good basic understanding of what is happening during each stage of the fermentation process. Now it is time to start putting that knowledge to work.

Fermentation Equipment

Before you can start to ferment, you first need to gather the equipment necessary to get you all the way through the process. There are many fine "starter kits" available through homebrew and winemaking supply stores that will include all of the basic pieces necessary to complete fermentation and prepare you for the next step. If you do not have a homebrew supply store near you, there are many such stores online that specialize in this type of equipment. Although we are focusing on fermenting for the ultimate production of spirits, and therefore there are pieces in some equipment kits that you will not require, we will discuss the equipment that is used in winemaking and brewing, as well, so you understand what these pieces of equipment are and what they are used for and you can decide which kit would be best for you.

Fermenter: This is a fancy word for a food-grade bucket. Because there are generally two steps in winemaking during fermentation, you may see this called a "primary" or "primary fermenter," meaning that it is used in the first stage of the fermentation process. They may have a loose-fitting lid or a sealed lid with a hole to allow the gases formed during fermentation to escape. Either is fine, although I am partial to a sealed fermenter, as it helps avoid surrounding air, which contains oxygen and contaminants that can spoil your wash. You will hear people talk about using trash cans or a host of other containers as fermenters, but you want to ensure that you are using a food-grade container if you are making food-grade spirits. If your intention is to make only fuel-grade alcohol, then obviously it is

not necessary to use a food-grade fermenter. A proper, food-grade fermenter is an inexpensive piece of equipment, usually under $20, so here is not a place to try to cut costs. You will generally want a primary fermenter that is at least 20 percent larger than your batch size to allow space for the foam that will build at the start of the fermentation process. For certain types of product, such as grains, molasses, or fruit, it may even be necessary to allow more space, as the layer of foam could grow to an inch or two. Using too small of a primary fermenter can lead to one heck of a mess!

Carboy: This is a piece of equipment that is not generally used in spirit production. It is used almost exclusively in winemaking, but is sometimes used in beer brewing, as well. A carboy can be plastic, but glass is far more common. If you have ever seen a five-gallon water bottle on top of a water cooler, then you have seen a potential carboy. In fact, many a home brewer has used a water cooler bottle as a carboy for their five-gallon fermentations. In winemaking, you will start by ferment-

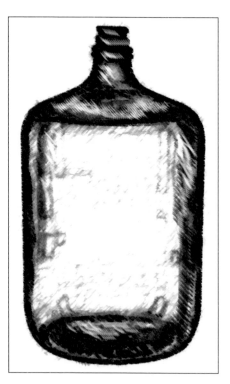

ing in your primary fermentation bucket, and then after the primary fermentation is complete (after the first few days), you will transfer, or rack, the wash from the primary fermenter into the carboy. The reason for this is that the size of the carboy more closely matches the volume of your wash, and because of the shape and small neck, you can greatly reduce the air space in the carboy, helping avoid oxygen and its deleterious effects. Some brewers will actually start their fermentation in a carboy specifically because of the ensuing foam buildup, as they can remove much of the krausen by connecting a hose to the top of the carboy that is routed into a container to collect the foam. By covering the open end of the hose with water, you allow gases and foam to be released into the container, while at the same time blocking air from getting back into the fermenter.

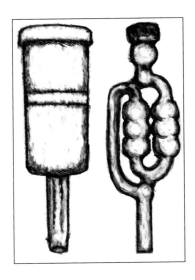

Airlock: An airlock, or vapor lock, is an inexpensive type of one-way valve that uses water to act as the control. There are several airlock designs, but all perform the same job, which is to allow gases formed during fermentation to escape while blocking outside air, which contains oxygen and spoilage organisms.

Hydrometer: A hydrometer is used to find the specific gravity, or density, of your wash compared with that of pure water. Pure water is considered to have a specific gravity of 1.000. If you take pure water and dissolve sugar into it, the density of the liquid will increase, and therefore the specific gravity increases. A hydrometer is a carefully calibrated instrument that has a weight in the bottom, and it will float in the liquid. Most homebrew hydrometers will have two or three scales, but all give you essentially the same information. The reason for the different scales is because of different preferences by the home brewer. The most common scales are specific gravity, potential alcohol, balling, and brix. Many European hydrometers will use the Oechsle scale, which is directly correlated to specific gravity.

Alcoholmeter: An alcoholmeter looks almost identical to a hydrometer, but the two do very different things. While a hydrometer is calibrated to the density of water and will read the density of a liquid relative to that of water, an alcoholmeter is calibrated to the density of pure alcohol and reads the liquid's density relative to that of alcohol. This may sound very similar in concept, but just because they look the same and are used in the same manner (i.e., floating the meter in the liquid to be tested), the difference in calibration means that there is no correlation between the readings. So if you think that you can cheat and use your hydrometer to obtain an alcohol reading in your distilled spirit, or your alcoholmeter to read the specific gravity, you are in for a surprise.

Test cylinder: Quite simply, a test cylinder is a tall, narrow cylinder that is used to hold a sample that you wish to take a reading of with your hydrometer or alcoholmeter. They can be made of either glass or plastic, but if you intend to use the cylinder for testing your distilled spirits, then you must use either glass or chemical-tolerant plastic. The clear plastic cylinders are usually made from acrylic, which is not tolerant to the high-proof alcohol that you will be testing. As a result, you can consider an acrylic test cylinder to be a single-use item, as it will be destroyed by high-proof alcohol. It may also taint your test sample, so it is simply best to avoid acrylic in the distillation process. Many inexpensive homebrew equipment kits will include an acrylic test cylinder. In this case, it is wise to purchase a separate test cylinder for your spirits testing.

Mixing spoon: Because you will be mixing ingredients in your fermenter, you will require a long-handled spoon. The spoon needs to be made of either plastic or metal, so that it can be properly sanitized prior to use. A long-handled wooden spoon may seem like a great, inexpensive option, but wood is too porous to be sanitized. They are great for cooking, where they will be used at elevated temperatures, but in the relatively low-temperature wash, it is too risky, as it can introduce spoilage organisms (such as bacteria) that will take hold of your wash and ruin it. Most homebrew equipment kits will include a plastic spoon, but they can certainly be found at any homebrew supply store and will usually cost only a few dollars.

Siphon: A siphon is used to transfer, or rack, liquid from one container to another. While a simple piece of flexible tubing can be used, a homebrew-style siphon has a couple of distinct advantages. Unlike a simple piece of tubing, a siphon will have a rigid cane-shaped piece of tube (known as a racking cane) that can be placed in your fermenter, ensuring that you reach the bottom of the vessel. On the bottom of the racking cane there should be a plastic tip, known as an anti-sediment tip. The purpose of the anti-sediment tip is to reduce the amount of sediment in the fermenter from being carried over during racking. Siphoning from one container to another is a rather regular occurrence, so this small investment will save you a lot of headaches (and likely a few foul words along the way). Most homebrew equipment kits include a siphon. Usually made with an acrylic racking cane and flexible PVC tubing, they are also available in a much higher quality version using a stainless-steel racking cane that is practically indestructible and chemical-tolerant flexible tubing.

Starting the flow of a siphon can be done a couple of ways. The most common, and obviously least sanitary way, to start a siphon is by sucking on it. A far better way is to fill the entire siphon with water, clamp it off by plugging the end of the hose with your thumb or by crimping the hose, place the racking cane into the liquid to be transferred, lower the hose into the receiving container (which must be at a lower level than the container that you are siphoning from), and release the hose. Because the siphon was full of water, it is "primed" and starts flowing immediately. This is an especially simple way to start your siphon because you can sanitize it, then run water through the siphon to rinse it. When you are finished rinsing the siphon, you can just clamp it off and it is primed and ready to go.

Thermometer: There are several styles of thermometers that are used in fermentation and some degree of preference when deciding which type(s) to use in your procedure. The laboratory thermometer is most commonly used for checking the temperature of the wash to ensure that you achieve the optimal temperature for pitching the yeast to keep your yeast happy. It is generally accurate and easy to read, but it does take a free hand to hold as it does not float. This brings us to the floating thermometer. A floating thermometer can remain in your wash throughout the entire fermentation process. This can be handy for checking the temperature of the wash during the fermentation process, but it has the distinct disadvantage of requiring the opening of the fermenter to check the temperature.

And, as discussed earlier, once fermentation has started, it is best to leave the fermenter closed to avoid the possibility of introducing oxygen or contamination from the air. So how do you keep an eye on the wash temperature during fermentation? Using a stick-on thermometer, such as those used in fish and reptile aquariums, is a great option. Although most aquarium thermometers will not show the temperature range that you will be working with when you ferment, most homebrew stores carry one with the correct range. These thermometers simply stick to the outside of your fermenter so you can easily monitor the wash temperature. While not as accurate as a laboratory or floating thermometer, they are extremely convenient and generally accurate enough for this purpose.

How to Use a Hydrometer

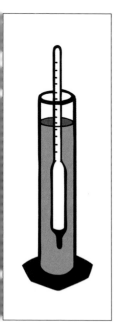

A hydrometer is a fragile and sensitive glass laboratory instrument that works by floating in a liquid at a specific level based on the density of the liquid. In brewing, the increase in density is generally the result of the addition of sugar, so we can use the hydrometer to gauge the approximate amount of alcohol that we will create through fermentation. In the bottom of the meter is a weight to help pull the hydrometer down into the liquid, and this is balanced with the weight of the meter itself and the air in the meter to ensure that it is only able to sink a certain distance into the liquid based on how dense the liquid is. In the stem, there is a piece of paper with the scale(s) that give you the information you need. To take a hydrometer reading, place a sample of the wash into your test cylinder and carefully lower your hydrometer into the sample. Do not drop the hydrometer, as it can hit the bottom of your test cylinder and break. Give the hydrometer a slight spin to dislodge any bubbles that may be clinging to it, as these bubbles can lift your hydrometer slightly, resulting in an inaccurate reading. Your hydrometer reading is taken by reading the number where the surface of the liquid crosses the stem of the hydrometer.

You will now need to adjust your reading based on the temperature of the liquid. Hydrometers are calibrated for a certain temperature, most commonly 60° F(15.6° C). This is important to remember, as the density of the liquid will change with its temperature. Take honey as an example. As you heat it, it will become thinner in consistency, or less dense. The same is true with your wash, and although it is not a noticeable difference to you or me, it is very noticeable to a sensitive piece of equipment such as a hydrometer. For this reason, you will need to know the temperature of the wash when you take your hydrometer reading, as well as the temperature that your hydrometer is accurate at. Most hydrometers will have this information printed on the paper inside them. A good rule of thumb is that for every 10° F from the calibrated temperature, add 0.002 to 0.003 to the actual specific gravity reading. For example, if your hydrometer is accurate at 60° F, and your wash is at 90° F, then you will add 0.006 to 0.009 to your actual reading (a 30° difference at 0.002-0.003 for every 10°). Some hydrometers will provide a more accurate correction table specifically for the brand and style of meter, but a difference of even 0.002 or 0.003 is less than 1 percent difference in your final fermented alcohol percentage, so it is certainly nothing to become extremely concerned about for anyone other than commercial operations, where that translates directly to the bottom line.

A hydrometer reading is of help to you in several ways, depending on when it is taken. You will usually take a specific gravity reading once you have mixed your wash and before adding the yeast. This reading can be used to tell you how much alcohol you will potentially create if all the added density is from sugar and if it all ferments out. This may sound like a lot of "ifs," but don't worry, it will all make sense as we continue through the fermentation process and take more hydrometer readings. Here is where a second scale on your hydrometer—the potential alcohol scale—can be very helpful. After recording your initial specific gravity reading, known as the original gravity (OG), you can look at the potential

A hydrometer reading.

alcohol scale to get an idea of how much alcohol this particular wash may create. The problem with having the potential alcohol scale is that it is commonly misinterpreted by novices as the actual amount of alcohol present, and when taking a reading after fermentation is complete, they will look at a potential alcohol reading that is often at or below 0 percent and they will think that there is no alcohol present, sending them into a panic. Just remember that this scale is potential alcohol, which is the amount of alcohol yet to be produced from when the reading is taken until fermentation is complete. Therefore, a reading of 0 percent means that there is no alcohol yet to be produced.

Similarly, those who do not understand the difference between a hydrometer and an alcoholmeter will sometimes use their hydrometer to test the alcohol content of a distilled spirit and immediately think that their meter is broken when it drops out of sight. This is because a hydrometer is calibrated to the density of water, which is much more dense than alcohol. To obtain the alcohol content of a distilled spirit, you need to use an alcoholmeter.

A hydrometer can also be used to confirm that fermentation is complete. If fermentation has slowed, or appears to have stopped, but you are not certain that it has completed, you can use your hydrometer to test for this. To do so, take a hydrometer reading and then wait at least 24 hours before taking another reading. If the second reading is lower than the first, then fermentation is not yet complete. If the reading remains stagnant, then fermentation is complete and you can move on to the next step in the process.

How to Use an Alcoholmeter

At first glance, an alcoholmeter looks identical to a hydrometer. Upon closer examination, however, you will see that the scales on the paper in the two are different. Adding to potential confusion is the fact that many hydrometers have a potential alcohol scale, and an alcoholmeter has, of course, an alcohol scale (actually, it is percentage or alcohol by volume, or %abv). However, the two are completely different, and one cannot be used in place of the other, even in a pinch. In fact, because alcohol is lighter, or less dense, than water, an alcoholmeter will not correctly read anything other than distilled spirits. To go a step further, an alcoholmeter will not accurately read distilled spirits that have had anything added to them. It is not uncommon for some distilled spirits to have a small amount of glycerin or other similar ingredient added to help increase the body of the spirit, as straight distilled spirits can be very "thin." Adding such a substance adds mouthfeel to the product, making it more palatable and denser. You know by now that this increased density will alter how high your alcoholmeter will float, resulting in an incorrect reading. So, to obtain an accurate reading of the alcohol percentage in your spirit, always test only the pure, unadulterated spirit.

The procedure for using an alcoholmeter is the same as for a hydrometer. Simply lower it into your test sample, give it a slight spin, and read the number where the surface of the spirit crosses the alcoholmeter.

As with hydrometers, most alcoholmeters are calibrated to 60° F. Unless your alcoholmeter came with a specific correction table, you can use the standard adjustment of subtracting 1%abv for every 5° above 60° F, or subtracting 1%abv for every 5° below 60° F, as shown in the table below.

°F	Adjust %abv
90	-6
85	-5
80	-4
75	-3
70	-2
65	-1
60	0
55	1
50	2
45	3
40	4
35	5
30	6

Table courtesy Brewhaus (America) Inc.

Other Supplies for Fermentation

Now that we have discussed the common equipment that you will need when setting up your home distillery, we need to discuss the other supplies that you will want to have on hand. For the home distiller, this list is comprised of just two categories—equipment cleaner and equipment sanitizer.

"Cleanliness is next to godliness" —Unknown

Equipment cleaner: This is more than soap and water, although you will definitely want to use those to keep your equipment generally clean the old-fashioned way. For obvious dirt, dust, or other things that you can actually see on your fermentation equipment, break out the hot water and dish soap. There is still no substitute for good ol' elbow grease. But be careful with your plastic fermentation equipment, as scratches can harbor bacteria and other nasties, which makes it extremely difficult to sanitize. It is usually the best course of action to replace badly scratched fermenters to avoid the headaches and tears of dealing with a batch that has been ruined by not being able to properly sanitize it.

There are several branded and proprietary equipment cleaners, and all homebrew supply stores will carry at least one or two good options. Unlike soap and water, equipment cleaner is meant to remove some of the organic and inorganic buildup on the equipment that you cannot see.

Equipment sanitizer: Not to be confused with sterilizing, which is both unrealistic and unnecessary in the home brewing and distilling hobby, sanitizing your equipment is a vital step that is often overlooked by home distillers. Whereas home brewers and winemakers are taught from the beginning about the importance of sanitizing their equipment as the basis for ensuring good results, many home distillers have not had this important step instilled in them. The thought process is that you are going to boil the wash anyway, which will kill any bacteria or other nasties, so it is not necessary. Unfortunately, that line of thinking can result in spoiled batches, and while it is true that you can at least distill out the pure alcohol, if your intention was to make a flavored spirit such as whiskey, well, that plan has just taken a backseat to trying to at least salvage something from all of your hard work. And it all could have been avoided by simply sanitizing your equipment. This is equally important to remember during the fermentation process if you must touch the wash. Any time that you will touch the wash, such as when you take a sample or obtain a hydrometer reading, it is imperative that you sanitize the equipment prior to it touching your fermenting wash to avoid contamination.

There are a number of options available to you for sanitizing your equipment and utensils, and it is not uncommon for a brewer to employ more than one depending on the stage of the process. For example, while it makes sense to mix up a gallon or two of sanitizer when starting a batch and you need to sanitize your fermenter, spoon, hydrometer, test cylinder, etc., it is not realistic to do this if you are just sanitizing a hydrometer or thermometer for a test during the fermentation. While there are numerous sanitizing solutions available, we will just look at those most commonly used in home brewing.

Household bleach: Yes, the very same stuff that you accidentally spilled on those new jeans, creating a new trend, is an excellent brewing equipment sanitizer. It is very inexpensive, handy (it is common in most households), and works well as both a cleaner and a sanitizer. Mixing one teaspoon (5ml) of household bleach in five gallons (19L) of water will provide approximately 15ppm of available chlorine, which is sufficient for sanitizing your equipment. So with how handy bleach is and its low cost, why consider anything else? Well, for starters, chlorine bleach can take a fair bit of rinsing to fully remove it from your equipment. Once your equipment has been sanitized, you will need to rinse the chlorine off of it using hot tap water (hot water from your tap is generally safe to rinse with. as it has been partly sanitized by heat). Also, chlorine is corrosive to stainless steel and copper, so its use in sanitizing your fermentation equipment is best kept to the plastic pieces. Finally, chlorine does not play well with many acids or other cleaners, so you do need to exercise caution when using bleach to sanitize your equipment. Never mix bleach with any other products.

Chlorinated sanitizers: Slightly different than bleach, these powdered cleaners/sanitizers are often proprietary, and because they are designed specifically for sanitizing, they often rinse off more easily than chlorine.

CTSP: CTSP is short for chlorinated trisodium phosphate. TSP is a very strong cleaner, and when chlorine is added, you end up with a dual-purpose cleaner and sanitizer. Another version is available as a combination of TSP with potassium bromide, which again is a strong dual-purpose cleaner and sanitizer.

Star San: This is a proprietary product from Five Star Chemicals that is offered through most homebrew suppliers. Its combination of phosphoric acid and dodecylbenzenesulfonic acid is biodegradable and does not require rinsing. It quickly sanitizes all homebrew equipment, but because of its acidic nature, extra care needs to be taken when using it. It is also rather expensive when compared with other sanitizers.

Metabisulfites: Often sold in homebrew supply stores as a sanitizer, neither potassium metabisulfite nor sodium metabisulfite are effective as sanitizers when added to water. To release the sulfur dioxide gas that will sanitize your equipment, these powders need to be added to an acidic solution. Simply adding them to water will create a very powerful-smelling liquid, but nothing more. Their use in winemaking is valid, as adding metabisulfite to the acidic wine will result in sulfur dioxide gas, which helps sterilize the wine must (the juice mixture) and can help preserve the wine.

Alcohol: Alcohol is an excellent sanitizer for your equipment, and it has the added benefit of being able to easily and quickly sanitize equipment, such as a hydrometer, without having to make up a whole batch of sanitizing solution. Using an alcohol-soaked piece of paper towel to wipe a hydrometer can be effective. And, because of its nature, alcohol will quickly evaporate from your equipment, leaving no residue, so it is not necessary to rinse. While isopropyl alcohol is considered the best to use for sanitizing, our good old friend ethanol works nearly as well. A concentration of 70%abv is optimal. At 100%abv the alcohol evaporates too quickly, which can result in some organisms basically "freeze-drying," only to be rehydrated when they come into contact with water. So keeping a bottle of 70%abv around for sanitizing can be very useful in brewing.

In addition to the sanitizers listed above, you will hear about iodine- and oxygen-based sanitizers. While these are perfectly acceptable alternatives, they are somewhat less common among home distillers.

It is important to note that the effectiveness of virtually any sanitizer will be directly related to the cleanliness of the equipment. So always make sure that your equipment is properly cleaned prior to sanitizing to ensure that your efforts are effective.

Clearing agent (fining): Clearing agents, also known as finings, are used once fermentation is complete to speed clearing of the wash. When we discuss clearing, we are referring to getting a majority of the suspended particles in the solution to drop and form a layer of sediment in the bottom of the fermenter. You can then siphon the cleared liquid into your kettle for distilling. I highly suggest clearing your wash prior to distilling, as distilling a cloudy wash can result in cloudy distillate. Although the yeast will not actually boil and be carried through the column as vapor, it is light enough to be carried on vapors that are created during distillation. The result can be a somewhat cloudy distillate with a slight yeast bite. By clearing your wash prior to distillation, you are removing this possibility.

In addition to contributing to a cloudy distillate, boiling the yeast can rupture the cell walls, releasing smells and flavors that will be carried across into your distillate. A cloudy wash can also contribute to foaming of the boiling wash, which will create other issues with the distillation process.

Clearing agents work on a positive–negative attraction basis. A clearing agent holds a strong positive or negative charge, depending on the type of clearing agent being used. You will select your clearing agent based on what you are trying to clear from your wash. If you are trying to settle something such as yeast, which has a negative charge, then you will use a clearing agent that has a positive charge. Yeast is very light and can take time to settle to the bottom of the fermenter, but by adding a clearing agent with a strong positive charge, you will attract yeast cells, and the increased combined weight will then drop out of solution much more quickly. Unlike brewing and winemaking, where there are a number of different things potentially in solution that we may wish to remove, and several clearing agents available to deal with them, hobby distillers are dealing overwhelmingly with settling out yeast. While there are several positively charged clearing agents available, two have become clear winners in hobby distiller's eyes.

Sparkolloid: This is a proprietary product developed by Scott Laboratories. It is a combination of diatomaceous earth, amorphous silica, and alginates. While there are both hot mix and cold mix varieties available, in home winemaking and distilling we use only the hot mix type. It is a tan-colored powder that is boiled in water and then added to the wash while still hot. Sparkolloid is very effective and will often clear the wash sufficiently in 24 to 48 hours. Its popularity is also undoubtedly due in part to its low cost when compared with other similarly effective clearing agents.

Two-part clearing agent: Different varieties of two-part clearing agent exist, but they are all a two-step process that uses both a positively charged and a negatively charged component. The most common combination is kieselsol and chitosan, although kieselsol and gelatin is also available. This is a great option when you need to settle out both positively and negatively charged particles or when you need an extremely fast clearing of your wash. The first part of the two-part clearing agent is added, usually the negatively charged portion, which will attract positively charged particles very quickly. After about an hour, the second positively charged part of the clearing agent is gently stirred into the wash, attracting both yeast cells and the molecules formed when the first part of the clearing agent was added. The combined weight of these particles is then sufficient to drop them to the bottom of the fermenter very quickly, often in 24 hours or less.

Anti-foam agent: As its name implies, this is an ingredient that is used to reduce foaming, either during fermentation or distillation. Anti-foam agents are certainly more commonly used during the distillation process, but can also be used in fermentation where foaming may be of concern, either because your ingredients lend themselves to larger, frothier heads of foam or because your fermenter is not substantially larger than your current batch size. Fruit, grain, and molasses washes often foam excessively and could outgrow the fermenter if sufficient head space is not provided. They will also tend to produce a large amount of foam when being boiled, which can cause grief throughout the distillation process.

Anti-foam agents work by altering the surface tension of the bubbles that form, causing them to break more quickly than if an anti-foam agent is not used. This reduces the buildup of foam on the surface of the liquid and reduces the issues that can come from foam buildup.

Water: Yes, I know that this is technically an ingredient in your wash, but given that it comprises 90 percent or more of your wash, it is a very important ingredient. Due to being such a substantial portion of your wash, it can impart its character into your finished product. So if you do not like to drink the water from the tap, do not use it to make your wash. While most municipal tap water is acceptable to use for fermentation, as is almost any water source that is safe for consumption, you also need to be aware of certain issues that can arise. The primary concern with municipal water is that it contains chlorine. If the chlorine levels are very high, then the chlorine can combine with nitrogen compounds in the wash to form chlorophenols and other compounds that can taint your batch. In these cases, you should consider using filtered or bottled water or, better yet, distilled water. And, seeing as you have a distiller at your disposal already, distilling water for your fermentations is a very viable option.

Now that you have your equipment, it is cleaned and sanitized, and you have your other supplies at hand, you can get on to the business of doing something with them. So let's get to making something!

Sugar Fermentation

Yes, I know that all fermentations use sugar. After all, that is what fermentation is. When I say "sugar fermentation," I am actually referring to the simplest of all washes, which is usually referred to as a sugar wash. As its name implies, the sugar wash is simply a combination of sugar and water. Because a simple sugar wash provides no nutrition for the yeast, you must either add a complete nutrient complex or use turbo yeast. I highly suggest a simple sugar wash as your first strides into fermentation, due to its ease and relatively low risk of mistakes. Because distillation is a two-step process—fermentation followed by distillation—this can help troubleshoot the process if your final product is not what you expected on your inaugural run.

The basic sugar wash:

Ingredients:
14 pounds granulated white sugar
6 gallons of fresh, filtered, and dechlorinated water
1 package of turbo yeast, sufficient for 6.6 US gallons (25L)
Clearing agent

Equipment required:
8-gallon or larger primary fermenter with tight-fitting lid
Airlock
Long-handled plastic spoon
Thermometer
Hydrometer
Test cylinder (optional)

Clean and sanitize all the equipment using equipment cleaner according to package directions. Bring two gallons of water to a boil and add to fermenter. Dissolve sugar, adding more hot water if required. Top up fermenter with a combination of ice, cold water, or warm water to obtain a total volume of 6.6 US gallons (25L) at a starting temperature of 100° F (38° C) or other temperature as noted on turbo yeast package. Float your hydrometer in the wash, or add sample to test cylinder (the advantage to moving a sample to the test cylinder is that you are able to wait until the temperature is nearer the calibrated temperature of the hydrometer before taking your reading. Record temperature and hydrometer reading. Add turbo yeast and stir vigorously until all nutrients are dissolved and no clumps of yeast remain. Place lid on fermenter, fill airlock halfway with water, and place into lid.

Aside from the numerous variables, such as the starting temperature and the specific turbo yeast that you have selected, you can usually expect to see some activity within 2 to 4 hours. That's it. That is about all there is to it until fermentation has completed. Once fermentation has completed, you can add your clearing agent, and once the wash has cleared you can proceed with distillation.

At this point, you can also add flavoring to the cleared wash without distilling. Adding a flavoring such as a specialty liqueur essence allows you to make many of your favorite styles of liqueur, from Amaretto to Irish cream to fruit schnapps. Of course, this will not offer the clean base character or high proof resulting from distillation, but is a completely acceptable option to some.

Non-Sugar Fermentation

We already know that yeast ferments sugar, only sugar, and nothing but sugar. So what is all this talk about non-sugar fermentation? By non-sugar fermentation I am referring to the fact that we are not simply dissolving basic granulated sugar in water and tossing in our beloved turbo yeast, like in the previous section. No, we are actually going to have to work for the sugar now.

Sugars are simply a short-chained component in things much larger, such as starch. Yes, you heard right, and no, that does not mean that you can steal your wife's laundry starch and turn it into booze. Starch, such as that found in abundance in potatoes, corn, barley, and a host of other foods, is an excellent source of fermentable sugar, if you are willing to go get them. These starches are just long-chained sugars. And yeast is too lazy to ferment starch, so you have to do part of the work for it by breaking the starch down into something that the yeast can consume. To do this, you require special enzymes to act as a hatchet, chopping the long chains into short ones. The enzyme that you need to use to break down the starches, or any long-chained sugar for that matter, is amylase enzyme. To complicate matters, there is more than one type of amylase enzyme, and their purposes and how they are used are different.

Alpha Amylase Enzyme

Alpha amylase enzyme is the heavy worker of the group. It breaks long-chained sugars down by chopping them into smaller bits. It is aggressive, rapidly breaking bonds of starch in the middle, producing random sugars (dextrins). It continues to break these chains down until they become chains of one, two, or three glucose molecules, which can be fermented by the yeast. This process is called liquefication.

Alpha amylase is obtained either from malted barley, such as that used in all-grain fermentation, or as a powder that is available at most homebrew supply stores. It is generally used at a higher temperature range than yeast can handle (130° F to 165° F, depending on the enzyme source), so liquefication, or mashing, must be done prior to fermentation.

Beta Amylase Enzyme

Beta amylase enzyme works by breaking small pieces from the ends of the chains. This process is known as saccharification. As you can imagine, such precise work takes time, which is why alpha and beta amylase enzymes work so well together. While alpha amylase is rapidly chopping the very long chains into shorter ones, beta amylase can break pieces off the end to create one-, two-, or three-chained sugars. Beta amylase will preferentially produce two-chained sugars, known as maltose. Its preferred temperature range is 126° to 144° F, but it can work for short periods (roughly 45 to 60 minutes) at temperatures above 150° F, after which it becomes permanently deactivated. Beta amylase enzyme is found in malted grain, but unlike alpha amylase, it is not available as a powder. But that's all right, as we have another enzyme that can do much the same job, and it is available from most homebrew supply stores in powdered form.

Gluco Amylase Enzyme (a.k.a. Gamma Amylase, a.k.a. Amyloglucosidase)

Yes, that is a lot of names for one enzyme. It is most commonly known as gluco amylase enzyme, but you will also often hear the name amyloglucosidase in certain circles. Rarely do you hear the term gamma amylase in the home brewing and distilling industry.

Gluco amylase enzyme works much like beta amylase in that it breaks the long chains from the end, essentially biting pieces off. The advantage to gluco amylase, however, is that it will preferentially create single-chained molecules of glucose, which are highly fermentable by the yeast. While this may not be the goal in brewing, where you desire some longer chained, non-fermentable sugars to give body to the product, in distilling you are primarily after the highest possible alcohol yield, as this body cannot carry over through the distillation process.

Because gluco amylase enzyme can work at slightly lower temperatures, and saccharification can be a somewhat slower process because gluco amylase breaks individual glucose molecules from the longer chains, it is often added at the same time as the yeast. This allows saccharification to take place at the same time that fermentation is going on.

Gluco amylase enzyme is available in powdered form through most homebrew supply stores.

Gypsum (Calcium Sulfate)

Gypsum is used to "harden" water and is helpful in achieving optimal pH for mashing. The enzymes mentioned above, in addition to others in the malt that are part of the mashing process, work best in a pH range of 4.2 to 5.8, depending on the type of enzyme. This means that a pH of 5.2 is optimal for mashing, and fortunately for us, this occurs naturally when your grain is combined with water. The addition of a small amount of gypsum is helpful in achieving an optimal mashing pH.

Iodine

Iodine is used to confirm that all the starches in your mash have been converted to sugar. This works because iodine will change color to black or purple in a solution containing starch. This test is not completely effective when the liquid is hot, so it is best to use a cooled sample for your iodine test. To do an iodine test, take a tablespoon of the mash liquid and place it on a cool saucer. Place one drop of iodine into the liquid and observe whether or not the sample changes color to black or purple. If there is a color change, then allow the mashing to continue until a repeated test shows no color change.

Alternate Mashing Method

With all of this said, there is a second method of mashing used in the distilling industry. Whereas the preceding method is known as a "cooker mash," because you are using an elevated temperature to quickly convert all starches into fermentable sugars, a second "no-cook" mashing method works at normal fermentation temperature without having to maintain the mash at an elevated temperature for an extended period of time. So why would you bother going through all the work for a cooker mash if you can just toss the grains into your fermenter, cover them with water, and pitch your yeast? Well, first of all, it is slightly more involved than that, and much of our alcohol is acquired from granulated sugar. But most importantly, the different mashing methods produce finished products with a somewhat different character, so preference is really the key here. The no-cook method is also most commonly used in "sour mash" recipes, where a percentage of the liquid remaining in the boiler after distillation is used in a subsequent fermentation. This liquid is known as "backset." There are a number of famous whiskies that use the sour mash process and probably an equal number using a cooker mash. So go through the recipes later in this book and compare for yourself. Experiment. Have fun with it, and you may just stumble onto something completely unique and wonderful. If you happen to make something that you don't like, there are always friends who are happy to take it off your hands, or you can redistill it into neutral spirits, opening up a whole list of things that you can do with it.

3. Types of Distillation

The evolution of distilling, (L–R): alembic, stock pot, "hillbilly style kettle" with worm, thumper, and reflux column.

The Evolution of Distilling

IF THE CHART above tells us anything, it is that home distilling has come a long, long way since it began. Distillation is believed to have started as early as 3000 BC. Obviously, this would have been a very crude form of the craft that we know today, and little, if anything, is similar to the methods used literally thousands of years ago. Today's distiller is informed, has far more sophisticated equipment and recipes, and a host of excellent quality ingredients available.

Another thing that you will come to learn from the chart above is that some of the drawings can be moved from one place to another, and it will be just as accurate. This is because there is no clear-cut order in which some types of equipment came about, and it is likely that different styles of equipment were developed simultaneously in different parts of the world. In addition, some styles of distillation that were once thought to be destined for the history books have recently made strong comebacks, most likely due to the renewed interest in hobby distilling that is being realized today. One thing that is certain is that the newfound interest is not likely to wane soon. The interest in hobby distilling is literally booming, both among home brewers and winemakers who find it to be the next logical step in their hobbies and those who have little experience but are highly interested in the hobby of distilling. The explosion of small-scale "micro" distilleries is clear evidence of this. How, you ask? Those are commercial businesses and have nothing to do with home distilling. That is not really true. You see, most of these microdistilleries are the result of a home distiller taking his or her hobby to the next level. And they are responsible for many of the unique and handcrafted liquors and liqueurs that you find on the liquor store shelf. Yes, they went legit and are making a living doing what they love. But it is safe to say that many of them started out right where you are now—tinkering with a new hobby. That is not to say that you will necessarily want to take this beyond a hobby level, but what it does prove is that you can let your imagination run wild. You can try new things—new methods, new recipes, different combinations of ingredients, different ways of aging your product. In fact, you have more flexibility than those commercial operations, because they must adhere to guidelines with respect to the different categories of spirits. They also need to appeal to a broad spectrum of tastes and cannot be as outrageous in their ideas, as they need to consider the bottom line. You, on the other hand, can do whatever you like.

As you already know, distillation is a process in which you boil a liquid, condense the resulting vapors, and collect specific part(s) of it to achieve your desired finished product. Sounds simple enough, right? But just as with fermentation, there are different ways to go about distilling, and they will yield very different results. This is because different methods of distillation offer a different degree of separation of the different vapors. Why then would you not just go with the method of distillation that offers the most defined separation so you can collect only the purest alcohol? Because if you collect only the purest alcohol, then you'll end up with vodka. There is nothing wrong with vodka. Many people like vodka, and it is by far the most popular of all types of spirits. However, I am sure that you have interests ranging beyond just vodka. And, if people were only interested in vodka, which is supposed to be "neutral" (color-less, odorless, and flavorless), then there would be no reason to use different recipes, as no matter what you fermented, you would end up with the same finished product. By distilling different ways, though, you are able to control what components of the wash you collect. This allows you to collect flavor and aroma compounds and make virtually any type of spirit or liqueur, from brandy to whiskey, rum, and, yes, vodka.

Distillation Methods

With all the different types of distilled spirits you would expect there to be many methods of distilling, but in fact there are only two that are commonly used—pot distilling and reflux distilling. This may sound oversimplified, but as you read on, you will find that it is also quite accurate.

Pot Distillation

Pot distilling is the more traditional method of distillation, and while it can be used to produce neutral spirits, it is generally used for making spirits such as whiskey, brandy, and other flavored spirits. This is because less separation takes place in pot distilla-tion than in other forms of distillation. While this is an older and considerably less advanced distillation method, it is still consid-ered to be the best option for producing flavored spirits. During the distillation process, you will bring the liquid in the kettle to a full boil. Because alcohol has a lower boiling point than water, it will vaporize more rapidly than the water in the solution, resulting in vapor containing a higher percentage of alcohol and lower percentage of water. The different flavor and aroma compounds have varying boiling points between those of alcohol and water and will therefore also boil off more quickly than the water.

A pot distiller does not have a tall column where you can further refine the vapor and instead takes virtually all the vapor that is produced and condenses it back into a liquid, which is then routed into a collection container. Although this sounds like a very crude and inexact method of distilling, by knowing the temperature of the vapor at all times and collecting only within a certain range, you are able to capture the alcohol, flavor, and aroma compounds that you desire, while leaving behind much of the water and other by-products formed during fermentation. This is where advancements in even the simple pot distiller have really helped the hobby distiller, as many of the new pot distillers include a thermometer, enabling you to see the vapor temperature during the entire process and control what you collect based on the changes in temperature.

Fractional/Reflux Distillation

Reflux is basically a fancy term for the repeated recondensing of the vapors that rise in a distillation column and are then returned to the system. This process is done in a tall column where components of varying boiling points will separate out naturally. Like pot distilling, the lower boiling point liquids will still boil more rapidly than those

with higher boiling points. However, in a column we are able to separate each of those components, or fractions, and collect only individual components. As the vapor enters the column and begins to rise, it will lose heat. When an individual component falls below its boiling point, it will condense and the liquid will begin to fall back down the column. This is called refluxing. This continues as the vapor ascends in the column, until at the top you achieve an individual, highly purified piece from the mixture boiling in the kettle. Your goal is to collect this pure vapor and condense it, leaving behind as much of the water and by-products as you can. While certainly not to scale, the diagram to the left shows how fractional distillation separates the different liquids based on boiling points, making it possible to collect a highly purified distillate at the top of the column.

Both to improve the effectiveness of the column and allow you to work with a much shorter column than would otherwise be necessary to achieve a high degree of separation, there are columns with additional cooling built in that will help force the refluxing to take place. These are known as forced reflux columns, although most people simply call them reflux columns. Some people also refer to these columns as fractionating columns, but all names refer to the same general type of column. While still in use on a very large scale, column stills have almost completely given way to reflux stills at the hobby level.

Types of Distillers

Stock Pot Still

While far from being one of the original distiller designs, the stock pot distiller can be quickly assembled using items that many people already have in the home. If you don't have the necessary parts, they can be purchased very inexpensively. Safety can be a serious concern for this type of distiller if proper care is not taken. The stock pot distiller also offers little to no control over what you will collect, so it is a very raw method of simply increasing the alcohol percentage from your fermented wash. With all of its short-comings, it is not a distiller that I suggest building or using, but with that said, it is certainly functional.

To build the stock pot still, you will need a large stock pot (at least a five-gallon (19L) preferred), a stainless-steel mixing bowl large enough to sit on top of the stock pot, and a slightly smaller stainless-steel mixing bowl that can fit inside of the stock pot with at least 1/4 to 1/2 inch of space all the way around it.

To use the stock pot still, you will fill the stock pot about halfway with your fermented wash and float the smaller stainless-steel bowl on top of the liquid. More of your wash can be added, but make sure that the mixing bowl remains several inches below the top of the stock pot. Place the larger mixing bowl on top of the stock pot and fill it with ice. You can now begin to heat your stock pot until it is simmering or boiling gently.

Because this system is not sealed, vapor is able to escape, especially if you are boiling very aggressively and/or if you do not have enough ice in the top bowl to condense all the vapor that is being produced. This can be a very serious safety risk, especially if your heat source involves an open flame. Alcohol vapor is highly flammable, so it is best to do this in a well-ventilated area and always be sure to have a fire extinguisher close at hand if you decide to try this method.

The general concept is that as the liquid boils, it creates vapor, which rises and makes contact with the ice-filled bowl, causing it to immediately condense. Because of the shape of the mixing bowl, the liquid will run down the side and to the bottom of the larger bowl, dripping into the smaller bowl floating below it on the surface of the liquid. This distillate is cold, so it will generally keep the liquid in the bowl from revaporizing, but even if it does vaporize, it will simply rise, hit the cold bowl, and be recondensed.

Unfortunately, this type of still does not offer the ability to toss away any of the early vapor, such as methanol or foreshots (these are the first bits to boil off and are generally undesirable in the final product), nor does it give you any way of knowing how much product has been distilled. Due to the safety concerns already mentioned, you certainly do not want to lift the lid to see how much distillate has been produced! Suffice it to say that you will simply have to estimate the length of time to distill and live with the drawbacks of this system. But, hey, it cost you little to nothing to build, so we have to expect there to be a negative in there somewhere, right?

Alembic Distiller

Probably the oldest true distiller design, the alembic still is definitely the fanciest-looking of all distillers, and they make great conversation pieces. But make no mistake, they are also fully capable, and they come in a large array of sizes, from as small as

1 quart (1L) to 10 gallons (40L) or more. These are almost exclusively handmade from copper sheet, so they are as unique as they are beautiful. However, they have two substantial drawbacks. First, just like the stock pot still, there is no thermometer giving you the ability to read the vapor temperature, although one could be added without too much difficulty. Second is the price. These may be works of art, but they are priced accordingly. On the plus side, you can see distillate being produced as it drips from the end of the condenser, so you can at least collect it in small containers and blend the finished product to your liking.

The "Hillbilly" Still

This is the backwoods version and is meant for large production, not premium quality. This type of distiller often has a kettle ranging in size from 50 gallons to several hundreds of gallons, and it is frequently heated over an open wood fire. They will sometimes have a thermometer built in, but more often than not no mind is paid to the temperature in the backwoods. The hillbilly type of still works much the same as an alembic still and is intended solely for pot distillation. To condense the larger amount of distillate being

produced, this type of still uses a long coil of copper, known as a worm, to condense vapor using the surrounding air as a form of heat exchanger.

Thumper Still

A thumper, also known as a "doubler" or "thump keg," is an added piece of equipment between the kettle (generally a simple pot still) and the condenser. This is an old "hillbilly" method, but it is making a distinct comeback in hobby distilling circles.

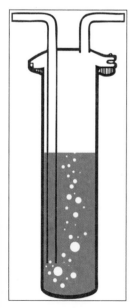

The name "thumper" actually originated because as the system heats, it makes a distinct thumping sound. Many modern thumpers do not do this, as they are made from heavier gauge materials than those used in the backwoods many years ago. A thumper can be made of any heat- and chemical-tolerant material, so you will see them made out of everything from glass mason jars to small distiller boilers, and even wooden barrels. It is also known as a "doubler," which can be somewhat misleading. Many people mistakenly believe that doubler means the still will double the purity of the distillate, but this is not the case. The term "doubler" refers to the fact that it acts very much like a second pot distillation, being similar to "double-distilling," or taking the distillate from your first pot distillation and redistilling it to increase proof and purity.

The concept behind a thumper is actually quite simple. You take the vapor that is coming off of your pot distiller, but before you condense those vapors, you run them into the thumper. The vapor runs through a tube that reaches very near to the bottom of the thumper, which is partially filled with liquid (water, fermented mash, or "tails" from a previous distillation). The vapor entering the thumper is quickly cooled when it enters the liquid, both condensing the vapor and heating the liquid in the thumper at the same time. As this process continues, the temperature of the liquid in the thumper will rise, and vapor will begin to rise from the liquid, exit to the condenser, and drip into your awaiting collection container. As the temperature of the liquid in the thumper nears the boiling point of alcohol (approximately 173° F or 78.3° C), it will begin to vaporize, making its way into the condenser and ultimately into your collection container. Because of the substantially lower temperature that this second distillation is taking place at, the distillate leaving the thumper will be of a substantially higher percentage of alcohol than the vapor entering the thumper. This is because at this lower temperature, many of the by-products and water will remain in the thumper, as they are well below their respective boiling points. Thus you have just run something very equivalent to a second distillation, all with minimal added time and heat being required, making this a far more economical option than double distilling.

This all sounds great. But what happens when the liquid in the thumper heats up to more than the boiling point of alcohol? Won't you then start to draw off more impurities, seeing the proof and purity of your distillate drop? In short, yes. This is why size is of importance when building a thumper. If the thumper is too small, or has too little liquid, it will result in a very short active life, as the liquid will quickly reach a temperature very close to that of the incoming vapor, and the incoming vapor will simply bubble through the liquid without being condensed, exiting the thumper exactly as it entered. In this case, your thumper is nothing more than a fancy-looking piece of useless equipment. The only way to combat the issue of having a small thumper is by reducing your heat input, but this will also increase the distillation time substantially.

If your thumper is too large, you may have other issues that can cause frustration. First, it is easy to put too much liquid into the thumper if the thumper is too large, and without substantial heat and a higher vapor temperature and flow, your incoming vapor will not manage to heat the liquid sufficiently, making your thumper act as a condenser. All the vapor from the distiller will be condensed and diluted by the liquid in the thumper. If the liquid never reaches a sufficient temperature, then you will not produce any distillate, potentially leaving you even further behind. But it is not as simple as just reducing the amount of liquid that you start with in the thumper because a large thumper will generally have a larger base area, meaning that less liquid results in a shallower liquid depth. A thumper works by making the vapor flow through the liquid in the thumper. The vapor naturally rises once it enters the liquid, so if there is insufficient liquid depth, then the vapor does not have enough contact time with the liquid to be condensed. The result is that the vapor quickly passes through the liquid and exits the thumper unchanged from when it entered, rendering the thumper useless. The final issue with a thumper that is too large is the surrounding contact area. Assume for a minute that you have a large thumper, but it is tall and slender, allowing you to place an appropriate amount of liquid into the thumper and still have enough liquid depth to be effective. This still leaves a substantial amount of surface area for vapor, leaving the liquid to be condensed on the thumper walls, and vapor that is condensed in the thumper never leaves the thumper—therefore, no distillate. The only way to combat this would be by increasing the heat level on your boiler, often substantially.

With all of this said, what is the optimal size for a thumper, and how much liquid should you charge it with? There are several factors in play, so the general rule of thumb is a minimum thumper size equal to one-third of the amount of ethanol in your wash, and a maximum size of twice the amount of ethanol in your wash. To calculate the amount of ethanol in your wash, simply multiply the volume of wash by the percentage of alcohol. For example, if you have five gallons of wash at 10 percent, you will take five gallons and multiply by 10 percent:

5 gallons (19L) of wash

x .10 (remember that percentage is always divided by 100 for use in calculations)

= .5 gallons (1.9L)

This is a rather standard-size wash and grain fermentation percentage for a hobby distiller and means that your optimal thumper size will be between 0.167 gallons (0.63L) and one gallon (3.8L). Remember that opting for the higher end of this range will result in a need for more heat on the boiler, which ultimately translates into a higher operating cost.

Column Still (Fractionating Still)

As mentioned earlier, any column still is in fact a fractionating still. How well it separates the fractions in your wash is dependent on several factors, including the diameter and height of the column, ratio of height to diameter, vapor production speed, and even the material that the column is made from. These are all intertwined, so it can be difficult to totally separate the discussion of one factor without considering how it affects another.

First we will talk about height. Height has possibly the greatest effect on the separation of the components than anything else. Quite simply, as the vapors rise in the column, they will lose heat, partly due to the cooler air surrounding the column, but even more so due to the exchange of heat with the falling (refluxing) liquid. As the vapor temperature drops below the boiling point of a specific component, that particular fraction will condense and begin to fall back down your distillation column, while the remaining vapor will continue to rise. This continues all the way up the column, with each fraction pulling itself out of the rising vapor when the temperature drops below its boiling point. As the liquid falls, it will gain heat from the rising vapor while simultane-

ously cooling the rising vapor (heat exchange). The process is assisted by having material in the column, known as column packing, that will stop the refluxing liquid from simply collecting along the walls of the column while the vapor rises in the center of the column. Column packing pulls the liquid away from the walls of the column, slows the liquid's descent, and essentially closes off parts of the path, forcing the vapor and liquid to utilize the same space. The falling liquid will continue to increase in tempera- ture until it again reaches its boiling point, at which time it will turn back into vapor and begin to rise in the column. Each time that this happens, the fractions become more and more defined. Components with similar boiling points will often not separate on their first cycle of refluxing, so the more times that this takes place the purer each fraction becomes. The number of times that this takes place is called the reflux ratio, and it is relatively equal to a similar number of distillations with a pot distiller. Components with the highest boiling point (which are nearest the bottom of the column, as they are the first to fall below their boiling point) will usually not gain enough heat to reach their boiling point before falling back into the boiler. As water and alcohol make up an extremely large percentage of the total volume of your wash, this leaves plenty of room for all the other components, mostly by-products of fermentation, to separate and remain in the distillation column throughout the process.

The goal in a column still is for your column to be tall enough to separate all the components, leaving only a single fraction at the top of the column, which you will then capture and condense. This is why column height (relative to the diameter) is considered the most important factor in purity. If the column is too short, then you will not get sufficient separation, and the resulting distillate will be of lower purity. If the column is too tall, then you will need to increase the speed of vaporization by adding more heat, which increases the cost of operating your still.

Diameter of the distillation column primarily affects the amount, or volume, of vapor that the column can effectively handle. Consider this at its most simple—your column has a defined and unchanging capacity (volume). It takes time for the separation to occur in the column, so if you feed vapor to it too quickly, it is unable to effectively perform this task. To increase the time that your column has to control x amount of vapor, you need to increase the capacity (volume) of your column. This can be done by increasing the height of your column, but most of us have limits on the reasonable workable height of the column. Ceilings often play a profound role in this. Also, as we are working with a cylinder, consider the volume calculation for a cylinder:

$$\text{volume} = \pi\, r^2 h$$

Did you notice that the radius is squared? This means that increasing the diameter can have a far more profound effect on the column volume than increasing the height by a similar amount.

In fact, increasing from a 2-inch diameter to a 3-inch diameter (standard hobby still size) will increase your column volume by 2.25 times! To get this same increase in volume, you would need to increase a 36-inch column to 81 inches. That is nearly 7 feet! Just imagine what this means on a commercial scale. An optimal height to diameter ratio is 15:1 to 20:1. If you fall much below the bottom end of this range, you may have difficulty obtaining adequate separation, resulting in lower purity distillate. Increasing the height to diameter much above 20:1 will result in the need for added heat to get vapor to the top of the column, which is quite simply an added operating cost on top of the added cost of material to build the column.

Column material is of importance because of heat transfer through the walls of the column. Without surrounding air being allowed to cool the walls of the column, there will be little to no heat loss in the column and therefore no separation. Too much heat loss can be an issue, as it will result in a demand for increased vapor production to get vapor to the top of the column. However, little to no heat loss means that you will not get adequate separation of the fractions in the column, and therefore you will draw off a lower purity distillate. Neither of these is a result that you will be happy with. For a properly designed column, it should not be necessary to insulate the column unless the distiller is being operated in the presence of windy or very cold weather, such as an unheated garage in the winter.

One important consideration with column stills is the requirement for column packing. To get the most out of the separation, it is extremely helpful to use some form of material in the column that will force the refluxing liquid to be spread out so that it does not simply run down the walls of the column. At the same time, we need to avoid only cooling the rising vapor nearest the walls of the column. This is done by adding some form of material to the column to move the vapor away from the walls, but it is important to still allow rising vapor the room that it needs to continue its ascent. In large commercial columns it is common to use "plates," which are designed specifically for this purpose. They come in many designs, but share in common the fact that they move both the vapor and refluxing liquid around relatively randomly.

Plates are not a viable option for small columns. Fortunately, there are several options that are suitable for hobby-size columns that are both inexpensive and very effective. The two most commonly sold column packing products for hobby distillers are copper mesh and ceramic raschig rings. Copper mesh is simply knitted copper wire that is rolled and added to the distillation column. It holds a distinct advantage over other types of column packing because it is made of copper, which will naturally react with the sulfur that is formed during fermentation. The resulting copper sulfide will remain on the copper, essentially stripping it from the vapor so that it is not carried into your distillate. However, the amount of copper required to react with the small amount of sulfur in your wash is quite minimal, so it can be achieved just as easily by adding a small amount of copper anywhere in your system, but most effectively near the top of the distillation column. Therefore, the distinct drawback of copper mesh, specifically the ability to keep copper— especially knitted copper—clean and free of tarnish, can be a never-ending job. For this reason, many people decide to use a different type of column packing and add some form of copper near the top of the column. Any form of pure copper is suitable for this purpose, but small copper couplings are a great inexpensive option and have the added advantage of being much easier to clean than knitted copper mesh.

Ceramic raschig rings are essentially tiny pieces of unglazed ceramic tubing that are usually the same size in diameter as they are in length (e.g., ¼ inch in diameter by ¼ inch in length). In small columns, a ¼ inch (6mm) is an excellent size to use. Ceramic raschig rings are much easier to keep clean than copper mesh. However, extra thought must be given to column design, as raschig rings are a "loose fill," meaning that they are hundreds of individual loose pieces that have no way of holding themselves in place in the column. While copper mesh will hold itself in place using friction between the mesh and wall of the column, this is not the case with any type of loose column packing. In such cases you will need a screen in the bottom of the column that allows the vapor to rise into the column unrestricted, while at the same time holding the column packing in place.

There are many other items used by hobby distillers as a form of column packing, including marbles, broken tempered glass, glass beads (such as those for making homemade jewelry), and a host of other things. However, the best column packing will have a very high surface area while at the same time not constricting the flow of vapor up the column and refluxing liquid. Too little surface area does not give adequate area for the liquid to descend on, while too little void space (open space between the bits of packing) can cause issues with the distillation. Both copper mesh and ceramic raschig rings offer a very high amount of surface area while still giving sufficient void space for the vapor and refluxing liquid to comingle and therefore should be at the top of your list when you select your column packing.

Forced Reflux Still

Now that you know all about column distillers, you may wonder why they are rarely used in distilling anymore, at least outside of extremely large commercial applications. Quite simply, column stills have given way to a newer type of distillation column—the forced reflux column. While technically these are column stills, the forced reflux column has the addition of some form of vapor cooling to help improve the efficiency and effectiveness to ensure that maximum distillate purity is achieved.

A reflux distiller with a band heater and end cap with a digital thermometer.

There are many designs of forced reflux stills, but they all share one thing in common, and that is that they offer you the control over reflux that is missing in a simple column still. This is done by cooling the vapor and returning a portion of the liquid to the column. In other words, you are controlling the reflux and what you allow to exit the system as distillate. Some designs work better than others, and some designs are simply meant to look different as a sales gimmick. Unfortunately, the latter often do not work as well as they are said to, leaving the user upset and searching for ways to modify their column to give better results.

Probably the most well-known and still most effective forced reflux still designs is the "cooling tube" design. In this design, tubes run directly through the column and cold water is run through them. The reason that this design is so effective is because the cooling lines are in direct contact with the rising vapor. When the vapor comes into contact with these cold lines, it is instantly condensed, forcing it to fall down the column until if vaporizes and rises back up for another shot at getting past the cooling lines. This will take place several times until only the fraction with the lowest boiling point remains. The goal in this type of system is to force the maximum amount of vapor to come into contact with the cooling lines or to flow very near them, so that the "coolness" that radiates from the line cools the vapor. The speed of distillation, and therefore the reflux ratio, is controlled by the speed and temperature of the cooling water being run through the lines.

In the past, most of these designs used two cooling lines, one in the middle to lower portion of the column and another directly above it near the top of the column. The drawback to this design was that the lower cooling line affected mostly the higher boiling point fractions, such as water, which would not reach the upper portion of the column anyway. This lower cooling line was actually only of value in a system that was drastically overpowered and producing more vapor than the column could effectively control. However, this was changed a few years ago by Brewhaus America, when they raised the lower cooling line to be near the top of the column and subsequently began crossing the cooling lines in an X

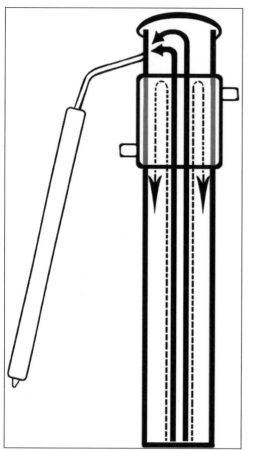

formation to increase the amount of vapor actually affected by the lines. They later increased the number of cooling lines in this formation to further improve efficiency. The result is that a very high portion of the rising vapor will either contact a cooling line or be affected by the cool temperature radiating from them. When this type of column is run properly, and the vapor does finally get past the cooling lines, it is usually of very high purity.

A system that is often marketed as an improvement on the cooling line design is one in which a cooling water jacket is placed over the outside of the column, allowing cold water to flow between the jacket and the distillation column. While visually more appealing, the system is far less effective than the internal cooling lines on anything but a very small diameter column, as very little vapor will be affected by the cold water. In fact, only the vapor at or very near the walls of the column will be forced to cool, leaving the majority of the vapor to rise to the condenser and exit the system. Increasing the lack of efficiency is the fact that the walls of the column are usually made of a considerably heavier gauge metal than that used to build cooling lines in the more traditional design, dramatically reducing the heat transfer rate. As a result, this is in essence just a very slight improvement on the simple column still, as little forced reflux actually takes place. The marketing for such designs often boasts increased distillation speed, but this is merely the result of a decreased reflux ratio, so the resulting distillate is usually of lower purity.

Because the systems above are, to varying degrees, controlling the rising vapor, they are commonly known as vapor
management stills.

External Valved Reflux

This is an extremely popular design that is widely used by
people building their own columns. As the name suggests, the
forcing of reflux takes place outside of the main column body.
The column rises from the boiler with either a 90-degree elbow,
or more commonly a tee fitting, at the top of the
column. A thermometer is installed at the top to
read the temperature of the vapor at the head (top)
of the column. The vapor, having nowhere else to go,
travels across the tee fitting to the reflux head. The
reflux head consists of a tee fitting with a short rise
on the upward-facing section. This section houses
a coil, usually made of copper, which has cold water
running through it. The vapor will come into contact
with the coil, and the refluxing liquid will then drip
straight down into the lower portion of the tee fitting.
This lower portion of the tee fitting will be capped
with a needle valve installed in the cap. The needle
valve allows the user to control the speed at which
distillate is collected, and in doing so also control
how much of the refluxing liquid is returned to the
column. Leaving the valve open entirely collects all
the distillate, with the only active reflux being that
which is inherent in any simply column still, while
closing the valve completely will return all refluxing
liquid to the column. While it does give complete
control over the reflux ratio, this type of system is
not without its flaws.

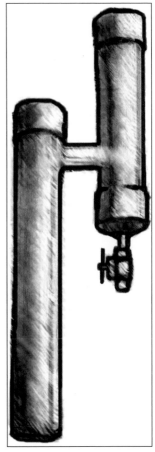

The primary issue with such a design is that the
lower portion of the tee fitting (where the condensate drips into) has a reservoir that holds the distillate to be
collected. All rising vapor that reaches the top of the column will
be condensed when it reaches the cooling coil, and that condensate

will then drip into the reservoir. This means that even the vapor requiring further purification will be mixed with the other distillate in the reservoir, reducing the purity of the final distillate to at least some degree. This can be remedied by replacing the tee fitting with a 90-degree elbow so that this collection area is eliminated.

Internal Valved Reflux

While fundamentally the same as the external valved reflux still, the internal valved reflux still is a variation in which the forcing of reflux is brought inside the main column. The result is a better, sleeker appearance, but this does not substantially alter the performance or basic operation of the column. With the internal reflux design, you still control your distillation with a needle valve, which controls the speed at which you collect your distillate. Even the actual design inside of the column is altered very little, despite the substantial difference in appearance. In fact, aside from a very

slight modification, that being that you must create the reservoir for the condensate to collect, you can essentially just move the reflux head of an external reflux still to the top of the column to create the internal valved reflux still. Because the design is fundamentally the same, it has the same benefits and drawbacks of the external valved reflux column.

Since the external reflux and internal reflux designs allow you to control your reflux and distillation through the speed at which you collect the refluxing liquid, these systems are generally known as liquid management stills.

A note on needle valves—the use of brass should be approached with extreme caution! While using brass is fine for water systems, it can be a concern in the presence of high-proof ethanol. In fact, according to the American Coalition for Ethanol (www.ethanol.org), soft metals such as brass may be degraded by high-proof ethanol. Any possible leaching of lead from the brass will contaminate your distillate.

Gin Column

Gin itself has gone through a change in production method over time. The earliest gins were made by pot distilling a grain wash and then combining the spirit with botanicals (juniper, anise, coriander, etc.) and redistilling in a pot still. With advancements in distilling, so came about changes in gin production methods. Today, most gin is made by redistilling a high-proof neutral spirit with the botanicals suspended in a "gin basket." The hot alcohol vapors extract flavor and aroma compounds from the botanicals, resulting in the flavorful finished product. This method is now used for many types of flavor infusion, including some brands of flavored vodka.

New column designs have been developed to reduce this infusion type of distilling to a single-step process and eliminate the need for a second distillation system. By placing the gin basket at

the head of the column immediately before the collection point, you can essentially create your high-proof ethanol and run those hot alcohol vapors through the botanicals all in one process. Some gin column designs are versatile enough also to be utilized as a forced reflux column or pot distillation column, simply based on how you choose to assemble the column. While this type of column may be slightly higher in cost than a single-use column, it is usually much lower in cost than the combined cost of all the different columns individually.

With that in mind, always consider the more versatile column versions when purchasing a distiller. Although today you may believe that your interest is very specific, as you advance in the hobby you will most likely want to try many different types of distillation and may come to regret purchasing a design that limits your options. This is not to suggest spending beyond your own comfort zone. However, if you must choose between a more versatile column, larger column size, or larger boiler, rarely will you regret the decision to put money toward a more versatile column design over either of the other two options.

Flute

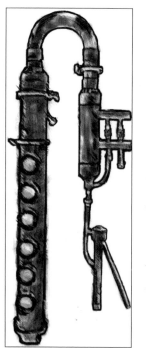

Flute columns are generally larger systems that are intended for increased production well beyond what the true hobbyist produces. While these systems are great conversation pieces and beautiful to look at, they are most suitable for large production rates, often distilling at more than one gallon of high-proof (90%+abv) distillate per hour. This makes these systems most suitable for small-scale commercial production, such as entry-level legal commercial distilleries. This level of production is also suitable for more advanced illegal moonshine operations.

In addition to the above designs, there are several other column designs and countless variations on them that are commonly used by hobby distillers. While some designs may give the user the feeling of having an even greater degree of control over the distillation process, every design comes with its benefits and shortcomings. An entire book could be devoted to all the different column styles and variations and still not touch on all the different designs being used. This is one of the wonderful things about hobby distillers—they are driven by a love for the hobby, and strive to constantly find improvements in efficiency or effectiveness. Unfortunately, many do not under-stand the underlying physical chemistry and make modifications that are ineffective or in some cases even contrary to improving a design. Ultimately, we must all live by the same laws of physical chemistry, and while we can work to improve the effect that we have on the vapor, every change that we make will have repercussions, whether they be positive or negative.

Photo courtesy Bob Rossi Jr.

A flute distiller on a 15.5-gallon keg, heated by a propane cooker.

Photo courtesy Bob Rossi Jr.

A flute distiller on a 26-gallon keg, heated with an electric kettle.

To Buy or Build?

You have decided that you are ready to be a hobby distiller. Your fermentation equipment has been assembled, and you have been researching all the different distiller styles and suppliers online. Maybe you have even been to your local homebrew store to check out what distillers they may offer, if any. But there remains a nagging feeling that you could save so much money by building your own distiller. How hard can it be, right? Well, that depends on how handy you are, what your access to parts is, and how much free time you have to devote to building the distiller (or want to devote to building your distiller!) versus having the equipment and just jumping into distilling.

Should you build your own distiller?

There are certainly many arguments for building your own distiller. Let's start by considering how easy or difficult it can be to build a distiller. Much of this depends on your own abilities, the type of distiller that you wish to build, and the material that you want to build it from. The kettle can be as simple as purchasing a used beer keg and removing the valve. The standard keg fitting used in the United States will actually mate up to a 2-inch tri-clamp ferrule, a pretty standard fitting that is easy to find. You can also modify a stainless-steel stock pot with relative ease. That was simple enough. Kettle, check! This is going to be a snap!

For those who are not extremely handy, you should stop here, find a retailer you trust, and purchase your distiller. This is not meant to discourage you or promote still sales for anyone. What it is meant to do is save you a lot of wasted time and money and ensure that you have a safe distiller. That last part is of utmost importance. Obviously you do not want to endanger yourself or your loved ones, and it is certainly not something that I wish to promote. However, if you have the skills either to solder copper or weld stainless steel, then it is worth at least considering the benefits and drawbacks to building your own distiller.

You have now decided that you have the ability to put the pieces together, but truly, how difficult is it to build a distillation column? Much of this depends on the type of distiller that you wish to build. It is obviously far simpler to build a basic pot still column than it is to build a forced reflux or gin column. So you must ask yourself what you need from the distiller and what types of distilling you wish to do, both now and in the future. Do not just build your column for today with the idea that you will just build another column in the future if you decide to expand on your home distillery. A lot of time can be spent on building, so it is something that you may not want to tackle again and again. Your best step at this point is to search the Internet for a design that you would like to build and find detailed building instructions. I do not suggest designing your own column at this point, as most people do not have the understanding yet to do so effectively, and that can lead to a lot of wasted time and money, as well as disappointment in the entire process.

The time required to build a distillation column is often underestimated. Once you have read over the plans and calculated how long it will take you to build your column, double it. Or better yet, triple it. No, I am not a pessimist. I am simply being realistic. Sure, if you went into commercial production, you could start firing those columns out in a fraction of the time, but one-offs are always much slower and more tedious. If you find that the real build time comes in less than your revised estimates, you will be pleased. But if you hit your estimated build time and are only half-done, then you will be upset and may even start rushing the remainder of the build, risking your safety in the process.

Now that you have your design laid out and know that you have the time to devote to building your column, it is time to start acquiring the parts that you will need to actually build it. Here is another point where many people decide to abandon the idea of building their own equipment and opt for purchasing a distiller. Access to parts can be a real eye-opener. In many cases, just purchasing the tubing needed to build your column can stop you dead in your tracks. It is not uncommon to be required to purchase a full 20-foot length of tubing, which can be very expensive, especially when you will only be using around 3 feet of it. And we are not dealing with inexpensive tubing. The most common diameter tube used for making hobby distilling columns is 2 inches, which most often requires a trip to a specialized plumbing supplier to obtain the tubing. If you do not have contacts that are able to get you just a few feet of the tubing, or at least a couple of friends to split the tubing with, you will be stuck purchasing the full 20 feet of tubing. Many of the other parts that you need will also only be available from plumbing warehouses, so the cost can add up very quickly.

Once you have considered all the points above—complexity in actually designing a distillation column, the often surprising cost of the parts needed to build the distiller, and the amount of time required—it often changes one's opinion on building. Suddenly those prefabricated distillers do not appear to be quite as expensive as they once did. This is often when people decide to build or buy based on their interest in tinkering. They decide to build their distiller simply because they want to, for the pure enjoyment that they get from it, and not because of cost or any other factors. Others decide that it is time to abandon the idea of building because, to them, it is simply not worth the hassle, and they decide to buy their distiller and put their efforts into distilling, not building.

One final consideration when deciding whether to build or buy a distiller is the legal aspect. While it is no more legal to build your own distiller than to purchase one, there is a difference in just who gets to know that you own a still. At the time of this writing, many of the distiller producers and distributors in the United States are required to report the sale of all distillers to the federal government. Those who are not already required by law to report the sales are required to maintain a complete list of the distillers that they sell and the purchaser's information for a period of three years, and they must surrender that information if it is formally requested. This does not exactly give a warm fuzzy feeling to the purchaser. Similar laws are in place in many other countries as well. This is a consideration that sends some people running to the parts store so that they can build their distiller, while others are unfazed. At the very least, it is a point that many consider when making the decision to build or buy.

Buying Your distiller

Having made the decision to purchase a distiller, you must now consider all the different designs, price points, materials, and a host of options offered in deciding where to purchase your distiller and exactly what to purchase. There are many producers of distillation equipment with sizes ranging from tiny countertop units to large commercial equipment. In addition to the relatively few major producers, there are many "micro" producers building and selling units on venues such as eBay or their own websites. So where do you start?

While I have nothing against the small producers, they have a couple of distinct disadvantages, in my opinion. Most importantly is the consideration of long-term service and parts. Things happen. If you drop your column and damage it, will you be able to get the parts that you need to get your distiller back up and running, or will you be stuck starting over completely? This is not a substantial concern to many people, but it is something that should at least be considered when narrowing your list of potential suppliers.

Another consideration that should be at the top of your list is the material that the distiller is built from. Many people jump immediately toward copper distillers, as they have heard that copper distillers are better and that they remove "something" that other distillers do not. This is both true and false. Copper does have a distinct benefit in that it will react with the sulfur formed during fermentation, essentially removing it from your distillate. However, the reactivity of copper is also a distinct drawback in certain types of distillation (mostly non-alcohol). With a copper distiller, you will have no way of removing copper from the system. Copper's other main drawbacks are cost and care. Copper is becoming increasingly expensive, and while it can be beautiful when kept polished, it offers no distinct advantage beyond that noted above.

The other material that is widely used for building distillation equipment is stainless steel. Stainless steel is strong, takes little care to continue looking beautiful, and is considerably lower in cost than copper. Fortunately, if you want the advantages that copper offers, specifically the ability to remove sulfur compounds, then you can simply add copper to the distillation column. It takes very little copper to complete this reaction, so anything from copper packing in your column to just a handful of copper at the top of your column will suffice.

Having thrown the advantages of copper to the side, you can now focus on finding the distiller design and price that you are happiest with, without regard for the material used to build it.

As stated previously, I suggest choosing versatility over size if your financial breaking point requires it. It is wonderful if you can have it all, but for many, that is simply not realistic. This is a hobby with a rather high entry cost, so it is wise to set a limit before you start searching for equipment to avoid sticker shock and regret from overpurchasing. It is very easy to start justifying different options, so go back to what you want from a distiller and how much you are willing to spend and stay within those parameters.

Having read the preceding information, you are already more educated than most buyers. This can be extremely helpful when comparing distiller designs and the figures touted by the respective sellers. Be wary of any company reporting questionable or downright unrealistic figures of distillation speed or purity, and especially a combination of these that does not seem reasonable. Remember what I said earlier—we all have to live by the same laws of physical chemistry. Nobody can change that. When a company claims to have a new magical design that drastically increases speed without a loss of purity versus similar size columns, I suggest looking elsewhere or at the very least proceeding with great caution.

Whether you choose to build or buy your distiller, do your research. Find the design that best suits your needs, both for today and the future. Do not overpurchase or overbuild, and most importantly, do not stress. This is a fun and rewarding hobby, and you just happen to get a pretty awesome product for your efforts, so enjoy the time that you spend on your hobby.

4. Distilling

IT IS TIME to take your fermented liquid and refine it. You have all of your equipment compiled, you have fermented a wash, and now you want to turn that into spirits. You already know that you will not actually be producing anything new in the distillation process, but in a way you kind of are. You are starting with a beer, for example, and finishing with whiskey. Technically you are simply removing water and some other minor components from the wash and collecting the alcohol, flavor, and aroma compounds, but it is hard to sit the two products beside each other and consider them to be so closely related. This is where the distillation process amazes me. Even with my long history in the industry, I am still fascinated with the distillation process. It is almost magical, how you can take a few simple ingredients like malted barley, water, and yeast, let it sit for a week or so, pour that into a kettle, and then watch this wondrous elixir drip from the end of your condenser. But there is a lot that goes into getting from fermenter to bottle. It is not simply a matter of dumping in the liquid, firing up the heat, and waiting for the distillate to appear.

Safety First!

The single most important consideration in the distillation process is safety. Never, ever forget that you are distilling fuel and that it is explosive. I cannot even say that you are distilling a product similar to fuel, as ethanol is widely used as fuel. From the gasoline that you purchase for your car (which could more accurately called gasohol due to the ethanol content), which often contains around 10 percent ethanol; to E85 fuel that is roughly 85 percent ethanol; to some fuels that are 100 percent ethanol . . . this is very explosive stuff!

This cannot be stressed enough. Exercise great care when distilling alcohol. Always have a fire extinguisher close at hand and never leave your distiller unattended during the distillation process. You would not walk away if distilling gasoline, and you should feel no less concerned distilling this fuel, either. The difference between distilling gasoline and alcohol is that, if there is a fire, water can potentially dilute the alcohol to a percentage where it is no longer flammable, whereas with gasoline it will literally exacerbate the problem. However, I never, ever suggest using water as your safety blanket, so always have a fire extinguisher handy and operate your distiller in a well-ventilated area.

Now that I have scared you sufficiently, I will say that in a well-built, properly sealed and operated distiller, under relatively standard operation and using a bit of common sense, the risk of a fire is almost nonexistent. Notice that I say almost. Do not become complacent or you will eventually find out just how dangerous this hobby can quickly become.

I would say that the three most common causes of dangerous situations during distillation are carelessness, improper building or damage to the distiller, and a plugged output. Hopefully the preceding information is enough to scare you out of carelessness, but invariably someone will start heating their distiller, walk away, and get involved in something else until it is too late. Once the distiller begins producing alcohol, you must be condensing the alcohol vapors. If the alcohol coming from the condenser is hot or is still vaporous, you must immediately turn off the heat to stop the production of alcohol. This is especially true if you are using any type of flame to heat the system, as the alcohol vapors can quickly ignite. Any time that you are using any type of flame to heat your distiller, you need to exercise extra care. Make sure that your distillate collection hose is kept a sufficient distance from the heat to avoid melting, as is your collection container. This may all sound like common sense, but unfortunately common sense is often not common enough.

If you have built your own distiller, then you should have pressure-tested all joints to ensure that the system is entirely sealed.

While I would like to suggest that if you purchased a distiller, it would have been done by the producer, this is too important to take for granted. If in doubt, ask the producer if they pressure-test the parts and how they are tested. No reputable producer will be offended, as they realize the reason for the questions. Do not be afraid to pressure-test the parts when you receive them, as well, in case of damage in shipping. Leaks in the system are extremely dangerous. You will not see or smell the alcohol vapor that leaks from the distiller, but they are very dangerous.

Although very uncommon, depending on the design of the system and a few variables, it is possible for the output of the distiller to become plugged. In such cases there is nowhere for the pressure to be released, and the pressure can quickly build to dangerous levels. For this reason, it is important that the distiller have some form of pressure relief. This can be as simple as using a bung (a tapered cork) in the top of the column that will pop out if pressure builds or as complex as a commercial pressure relief system with a preset bursting pressure. Under normal operation, your distiller will have almost no pressure buildup, so even a few psi will be a sign that something is wrong. Of course, just as a leak in the system does, when a pressure relief of any kind is tripped, you will be filling the air with dangerous alcohol vapors. Again, do not leave your distiller unattended so that, if necessary, you are able to quickly shut down the heat to the distiller and be prepared for any problems.

Heating Your Distiller

In order for distillation to take place, you must heat the liquid in the kettle until it is boiling. This can be done with any suitable source of heat, each with their own individual benefits. It is true that you could literally run your distiller over a wood fire, like many old-time moonshiners did (and some still do!), but aside from very large systems, this is not generally the best course of action. It is also the least controllable heat form, and for optimal results you want maximum control over the process, and that starts at the bottom with your heat source. If your heat source cycles on and off or is otherwise inconsistent in the amount of heat that it produces, then you will have a very difficult time getting good results. As the heat level changes, so does the speed of the boil, and while the temperature of the liquid will not change (boiling is boiling—your liquid will never exceed its boiling point unless under pressure), the speed at which vapor is being produced most certainly will. Without consistent vapor production, you will find it very difficult to have a smooth distillation run.

External Heat

This covers virtually any heat source that heats the kettle from the outside, including a wood fire. Due to the lack of control mentioned above, we will not discuss it further. The greatest advantages to external heat are cost of equipment and ease of use. Their biggest drawback is efficiency. With any external heat source, the heat must travel through the walls of the kettle before heating the liquid. Each metal has a "heat transfer rate," which is basically the speed at which heat passes through the metal. Copper has the highest heat transfer rate of the metals commonly used to build a kettle, however, aluminum and stainless steel also boast rather high heat transfer rates, as well. As you can imagine, the faster the heat transfers through the metal, the more efficient the system will be.

Common forms of external heat for operating a distiller are a household stovetop, electric hotplates, and propane cookers (turkey fryers and Cajun cookers). Stoves are not especially portable, limiting where you are able to distill, and with a tall reflux column they are often simply not a viable option. Electric hotplates have the advantage of being used anywhere that you have a standard power supply and are easily controlled rather precisely, making it simple to find the optimal heat level and repeat the process every time you distill. However, most people in North America do not have easy access to anything more than 110V power, limiting the hotplate options to a maximum of around 1500W. This amount of heat is not substantial enough for large kettles or columns, although a 10-gallon kettle is the maximum weight that can be used on most hotplates, raising concern over stability of the system. Induction hotplates, while very efficient, require that the metal used to make the kettle be compatible with induction cooking. This leaves propane cookers. They have the benefit of having plenty of heat to throw at the distiller, but they must be used in a well-ventilated area, and with the open flame you must take extra care during operation. Many propane cookers have reasonable heat control, allowing you to increase the heat level and reduce the heat-up time, as well as bring the heat to an optimal level for the distillation process. Most of these cookers are robust enough to handle the weight of a 15-gallon keg quite easily, making them a very suitable option for larger stills.

Internal Heat

Just as the term suggests, this form of heat is *inside* your boiler. It usually requires the addition of some form of coupling or attachment that will allow you to add a heating element that will be submerged in the liquid. While this is the most efficient method of heating your still because there is no metal for the heat to pass through, it has a large downside as well. With an internal heating element (such as a water heater immersion element), you are adding a substantial amount of heat to a small surface area, whereas with an external heat source your heat will be spread over the entire base of the kettle. As a result, the likelihood of scorching your wash and/or burning off some of the more delicate flavor and aroma compounds is much greater than with an external heat source. One way to reduce this risk is to increase the number of internal heating elements while reducing their individual wattage. This means possibly adding two 750 watt heating elements instead of one 1500 watt element. The result is an instant reduction of 50 percent in the heat density and a reduced risk of the issues that accompany high heat density.

A common, extremely effective, and efficient method of heating in food manufacturing is the steam or pressurized water jacket. This type of heat surrounds a large portion of the kettle, basically wrapping it in steam or high-temperature pressurized water. The result is a much more gentle form of heat that is also highly efficient. Unfortunately, this requires a special type of kettle with a heating jacket, which is not practical for most hobbyists.

Pot Distilling

What could be easier that traditional pot distillation, right? I mean, you just pour the wash into the kettle, heat, and out comes your distillate. It has worked for hundreds of years, so it can't be that difficult. This is true, but just what are you collecting if you do not pay close attention to the details? While distillation is a rather simple process—the liquid vaporizes, and you capture and condense the vapor—what you do to control what you collect makes all the difference in the world to your finished product. Not only does it make a difference in the taste and smell of your spirit, but it also affects the safety of it. With pot distilling, we are intentionally trying to collect more than just alcohol. Pot distilling of spirits is most often used when flavored spirits are being produced, so we are trying to capture all the good flavor and aroma compounds while discarding the bad by-products of fermentation such as methanol, fusel alcohols (also known as fusel oils), and other alcohols. These by-products that are formed during fermentation are called congeners. Your goal as a pot distiller is to collect the alcohol and "good'"congeners that contribute positive flavor and aroma compounds, while leaving behind all the "bad" congeners that impart bad flavors, solvent character, and an unruly burn on the tongue. Seeing as most of these congeners boil in a similar temperature range as our ethanol (the "good" alcohol) and our "good" congeners, it requires careful attention to what is going on in the distillation process at all times and often multiple distillations to achieve the smoothness and character that we desire. With each distillation through a pot still, you will increase the removal of congeners, but along with that are flavor and aroma compounds that, if removed, will leave you with a near-flavorless spirit. It is a great balancing act—trying to collect as much of the good and as little of the bad so that you have a flavorful spirit with as little "burn" and "next-day effects" as possible.

Before we get too far into the distillation process, let's discuss some of the congeners formed during fermentation.

Methanol (wood alcohol): When you hear of someone going blind from drinking moonshine, this is undoubtedly the culprit. While methanol actually has a use, it is in industry and most definitely not in your spirit. Methanol is a poison that has the ability to permanently destroy the optic nerve. It is one of the by-products commonly formed in small amounts during certain types of fermentation and also occurrs naturally (again in very small amounts) in some foods that we eat every day, such as some fruit juices. Fortunately, with a little bit of care, methanol is rather easily separated from the other compounds in our wash and thus from our distillate.

Fusel oils and other alcohols: These are generally less of a danger than methanol, but are also responsible for much of the "nail polish remover" character in distilled spirits, and much of the "morning after" effects. While they are not generally considered to be toxic, they are responsible for a bad flavor or aroma in the distilled spirit.

Suddenly this simple little pot distillation has become considerably more complex, hasn't it? Not to worry—by paying careful attention to the temperature at the head of your distiller, you will have a fairly accurate idea of what the vapor contains, and therefore whether or not you wish to discard the vapor, collect it for consumption, or collect it for addition to a subsequent batch. This is where pot distillation really becomes almost an art form, and in many ways it can be more difficult than reflux distillation, where we will work to pull one single compound from our mixture. Fortunately, we have reflux distillation as a backup, or additional pot distillation runs, so your worst-case scenario is having to redistill your spirit into a neutral product (vodka). Never throw out your distillate simply because you are unhappy with the results! That is literally pouring money down the drain.

Photo courtesy Will Collins

A pot distiller being operated in a garage.

To gain an understanding of why you are performing certain tasks at different points through the distillation, it is very helpful to know what is taking place throughout the process. This means knowing what components you can generally expect to be collecting as the temperature increases.

Before I break down the general temperature ranges used as a guideline for what to collect and not to collect when pot distilling, it is important to note this difference between pot and reflux methods. Many people will start with reflux distillation and are used to having a rather stationary temperature at the head of the distillation column. Then, when they venture into pot distillation, they become concerned because the temperature does not remain steady at the roughly 173° F (78.3° C) that they are accustomed to with reflux distillation. When we review the reflux distillation process, you will understand why the temperature does not generally change throughout most of the process, but with pot distillation, this is not the case. With pot distilling your temperature will increase. Again, if you are paying attention to the thermometer at the head of your pot distiller, it will not hold steady at one temperature throughout the process. Because the components with lower boiling points will boil off earlier, your mixture will gradually gain a higher overall boiling point as you draw off your distillate.

Photo courtesy Bob Rossi Jr.

Many people are also concerned when no change in temperature is showing on their thermometer, despite the wash obviously heating. This is because you are reading the vapor temperature and not the liquid temperature, and until your liquid reaches the boiling point for a component, nothing is vaporizing. Of course, once you reach that critical temperature, the vapor rises to the head of the still and the thermometer reading suddenly jumps from the ambient air temperature to that of the vapor that has found its way to the top. This usually means an almost instant increase from around 70° F (21° C) to roughly 150° F (65° C) as methanol, which has the lowest boiling point in your wash, begins to boil. The fact that methanol is the first component to boil off is helpful, as it makes it a simple process to remove nearly all the methanol by collecting this first distillate and discarding it.

Now it is time to learn the lingo, what it refers to, and what to collect.

Making the Cut

The points at which you start and stop collecting the distillate is known to distillers as "making cuts." The different cuts listed below are guidelines only. Use smell and taste to decide where to make your cuts, and remember that you are always able to redistill. So do not be afraid of making mistakes. Pot distilling can take some practice. By collecting in small amounts, you can also minimize mistakes that will require redistilling.

Foreshots (up to 176° F (80° C)): These are the first parts of the wash to come off during the distillation process. They consist of methanol and other volatiles, such as acetone and aldehydes. These are poisonous compounds that you want to separate from your distillate and contain very little ethanol, so simply collect and discard them. Never allow them to mix with the alcohol that you plan to consume. If you accidentally collect more than intended, toss it! It is simply not worth the headaches (literally) or safety. Foreshots are nasty and will taint your finished product, so it is not worth trying to cheat to save a few pennies worth of alcohol.

Heads (over 176° F (80° C) and up to 196° F (91° C)): Here comes the high-proof stuff. Heads are made up primarily of ethanol, but will still contain some congeners. They are usually 80%+abv. It is a good idea to collect the heads separately from the next stage, as you can combine them based on your own tastes. Some distillers will collect the heads and middle run together, while others will collect the heads separately and redistill them later into a more neutral spirit. There is no right or wrong here, but what you decide will definitely affect your finished product, so it is best to collect the heads in their own container for now and make the decision after you have completed your distillation. In fact, collecting the heads in a few smaller containers will help, as you may find that the latter part of the heads are perfectly acceptable in your finished product, while the first part is better being separated and redistilled.

Middle run/hearts (196° F (91° C) to 203° F (95° C)): This is what you came to do. You are now collecting the bulk of the distillate that you will be keeping as drinkin' alcohol. The middle run will have fewer congeners and be less harsh than the heads and will start at around 80%abv, dropping down to around 60-65%abv. Some people will continue to collect all the way down to 40%abv, but regardless of what you decide in this respect, it is advisable to collect in multiple small containers so that you can keep only the best, cleanest-tasting distillate for drinking or aging. Smell and taste each container to decide where you want to make your cut and keep a larger container for the final blending.

Tails (over 203° F (95° F)): As the name suggests, tails are the last bit of the run that are of any value. Tails contain the last bit of ethanol and are just collected to avoid wasting the alcohol that you created during fermentation. They will have a constantly decreasing amount of usable alcohol and an increasing congener content. Collection will generally stop at around 207° to 208° F (97° to 98° C). The tails are not kept as drinkable alcohol, but collected separately, often combined with all or part of the heads (if the heads are not included in your final distillate), and redistilled as neutral spirits.

With experience, you will likely find yourself relying less and less on temperature and more on your taste buds and nose when making the cuts above. Always collecting in multiple small glass containers will afford you the luxury of blending all the good spirits together while keeping the harsher or less favorable flavored spirits separate. Only use glass or ethanol-tolerant plastic to collect your distillate. Ethanol and many plastics do not get along well. Just place some 95%abv ethanol in a standard acrylic homebrew test cylinder and see what happens. The ethanol will destroy the acrylic and taint the ethanol in the process. Glass is always the best option, and as luck would have it, pint-size glass canning jars are both inexpensive and a great size for collecting your distillate.

Your First Distillation

This is one of the most exciting moments in the hobby. You have completed your first fermentation, your wash has been cleared, and you are ready to create your masterpiece. Unfortunately, this is also the most nerve-wracking moment in the hobby. Fear of messing everything up fills your mind. This hobby, which started out sounding so simple, now seems so involved. There are so many places to make mistakes. What if you don't get all the methanol out? What if it tastes awful?

Relax. Take a breath, realize that you have been reading and learning what to do and what not to do, and lastly, remember that in the worst of situations, you can always redistill your spirit, so there is nothing to get worked up about. So let's take baby steps, and everything will be fine.

Step 1: Ferment and clear your wash. This has been covered well enough already, so it is not necessary to go into great detail again. Simply ferment your wash and allow it to clear naturally or use a clearing agent to do so more quickly. I highly advise clearing the wash to reduce the risk of scorching material to the bottom of your kettle. Clearing is absolutely required when using internal heating elements to heat your still.

Step 2: Transfer the wash to your kettle. While you can use a funnel and simply pour the wash from your fermenter to your kettle, this will also drudge up the sediment and transfer it along with the clear liquid. It is far better to transfer the wash using a siphon, which makes it much easier to move just the clear liquid, leaving behind all the sediment on the bottom of the fermenter. Never fill your kettle to more than 80 percent of its total capacity! This extra space is needed for expansion and potential foaming that may occur during heating and boiling. Overfilling your kettle can create issues that will be extremely frustrating. To reduce issues associated with foaming, it can be very helpful to add an anti-foam agent to the wash.

Step 3: Complete the assembly of your distiller. Hopefully your distiller came with instructions, but regardless, this part should be rather straightforward. Drawings are provided in the Resources section for several popular distiller styles, just in case. You will place the pot still column onto the kettle and ensure that it is fully sealed. When vapor starts being produced is not a good time to find out that your distiller is not sealed.

Step 4: Start heating the still and be patient. Depending on the heat source and size of your wash, the heating process can take up to a couple of hours. It can be tempting to turn the heat up to the maximum to get the still producing as quickly as possible, but this is not always a wise decision. This is especially true when using certain types of propane cookers. These cookers can be capable of producing a very large amount of heat, and while they can get your wash boiling rather quickly, they can also put out enough heat to damage the bottom of your kettle and scorch any sediment that may have been carried across when transferring the wash. Trying to rush any part of the distillation process will usually show in the finished product, while patience will be rewarded. Now that you have started heating your wash, you should not leave the still unattended until the distillation process is complete.

Step 5: Start running your cooling water. While you do not necessarily have to start running your cooling water immediately after you begin heating your still, it is imperative that you start running cooling water into your condenser before any vapor starts being produced to avoid an extremely dangerous situation.

Distillate as it comes from a condenser.

Step 6: Remove and discard the foreshots. If you have a thermometer in the still head, you can use the vapor temperature as a guide. Once vapor starts to appear, the temperature will suddenly spike, and a few moments later you will see drops of distillate begin to flow into your collection container. Continue to watch the temperature until it reached 175° to 176° F (79.5° to 80° C), or until you have collected at least 4 ounces (125ml) of distillate.* Even if the temperature has risen to above 175° F (79.5° C), continue collecting until you have at least 4 ounces (125ml) of foreshots. Do not be afraid to discard a little bit more of the first distillate. The total cost in doing so is literally pennies, and your finished product will often be improved by doing so. Discard the foreshots. They are poisonous, so there is no reason to keep them.

Step 7: Start collecting the heads. Change your collection container and begin collecting the heads. If you are watching the temperature, it should now be over 175° F (79.5° C). The speed at which distillate is coming from the condenser will have increased, and will now likely be a medium to fast drip, but should not be a trickle. Continue to collect the heads in pint-sized glass jars until the temperature

* Note: The volume of foreshots is based on a five-gallon wash size. You must adjust this volume based on the size of your wash to ensure that all the foreshots are removed.

rises to 195° to 196° F (90.5° to 91° C). It is helpful to mark each jar with "heads" and number them as you draw them off. Although you will use your nose and taste buds to decide which, if any, of these jars will be included in your finished product, numbering the jars will help you get a good feel for the changes in the distillate as the process progresses. It is also a good idea to test the alcohol percentage/proof of the distillate as the process progresses. Many distillers use the alcohol percentage as a guide instead of temperature or use both to be more exact in where they want to make their cuts.

This is where a distiller's parrot can be a very helpful tool. A distiller's parrot is connected between the condenser and collection container so that the distillate flows through it on its way to your container. The parrot holds your alcoholmeter, allowing you to take real-time readings of the alcohol percentage as the distillate is being produced. While the readings in a parrot are slightly inaccurate due to constant blending of the distillate, they are generally more than sufficient for deciding on when to make your cuts. Because of this blending, and to avoid any contamination from the foreshots, always collect your foreshots in a separate container before attaching your parrot. Generally, you will find the heads to be over 80% abv (160 proof).

Step 8: Collect the hearts. Now it is time to start tasting! Yes, you can use your nose and taste buds with the heads, but especially at the start of the heads you may find this to be less than pleasant. Once the temperature hits around 195° to 196° F (90.5° to 91° C) and/or the alcohol percentage drops below 80%abv (160 proof), it is time to start collecting the hearts. Change your container to a new container marked "hearts," and just as you did with the heads, number them. The distillate will be coming out more quickly now, as a very fast drip or even a slow trickle. This can result in a slightly less accurate reading on your alcoholmeter if you are using a distiller's parrot, as there is a noticeable flow from the bottom of parrot, where the distillate enters, to the top, where it is being drawn off. It is still generally sufficiently accurate to make the cuts between heads, hearts, and tails, as these cuts are not usually extremely precise.

Photo courtesy Bob Rossi Jr.

You can run an alcoholmeter test as distillate is produced.

Continue collecting the hearts until the temperature rises to around 202° F (94.5° C) and/or the percentage alcohol drops below 65 percent (130 proof). If you want to ensure that you have a very clean middle run that will not require a second distillation, then do not be afraid to stop collecting the hearts slightly earlier. This will mean that you have slightly less volume of hearts and a little bit more tails, but the tails can always be added to a subsequent batch to avoid wasting any of the ethanol that they contain.

Step 9: Collect the tails. Change your collection container and begin collecting the tails. Most of the ethanol has been collected by this point, but there is still a little bit remaining. The point of collecting the tails is to avoid wasting this bit of alcohol. Continue collecting until the temperature rises to 207° to 208° F (97° to 98° C) or until taste and smell reveal little to no remaining alcohol.

Step 10: Shut down the still. Turn off the heat. DO NOT TURN OFF THE COOLING WATER! Just because you have turned off the heat does not mean that there is no vapor being produced. The liquid remaining in the kettle is still very hot and well above 173° F (78° C)—the boiling point of ethanol. That means that if there is any ethanol remaining in the kettle, it will continue to rise and make its way into the condenser. Keep the cooling water to the condenser running until you are certain that there is no more vapor being produced, as even a little bit of alcohol vapor in the air can be extremely dangerous. As soon as you are sure that no more vapor is being produced, you should remove the thermometer from the top of your still head or loosen the still head to allow adequate airflow back into the distiller. Just as expansion takes place when heating the still, when the still is cooling, the vapor inside of it will condense. Without adequate airflow, the still can literally implode! Once the still is cool enough to handle, you can remove the still head completely and dump the liquid remaining in the kettle (or keep a portion of it for use as backset, if you are running a sour mash recipe). Wash and rinse your distiller as per the manufacturer's recommendations.

Step 11: Blending. Depending on how you have made your cuts, you may wish to blend some of the heads with the hearts, or maybe you are pleased with the hearts that you collected and you want to keep all the heads separate. Either is fine, and your decision will depend on

the flavor and aroma of each container that you collected. If you decide
to keep the heads separate, you may either use this part of your distillate
as it is, add flavoring to it, or combine it with your tails and redistill.
Another option is to add the heads and tails to your next run. The choice
on this is yours.

Step 12: Aging and cutting. Once you have blended your final distillate to your liking you need to decide if you will age the spirit or
leave it "raw." Aging your spirit will allow the harsh bite of the distillate to mellow, and the flavors will become more complex. However,
not everyone prefers this character, so the choice is ultimately yours.
If you do decide to age your spirit in oak casks or with alternatives
such as oak chips, oak staves, or another type of wood, you will generally want to age your spirit at just over 60%abv (120 proof) and cut the
spirit (dilute it) after it has been aged.

Cutting, also known as "proofing down," is a fancy way of saying that you are diluting your distillate. It is a very simple process
of just mixing water with your spirit. There are a couple of reasons
to cut your spirit. First, reducing the alcohol percentage makes the
product noticeably smoother, reducing the bite and harshness of a

120 proof spirit. The second reason to cut your spirit is that aroma compounds are more easily released at this lower proof, resulting in a more aromatic spirit.

Second distillation

It is very common in pot distilling to redistill your spirit to obtain a more refined product. The advantage to multiple distillations is that it improves the removal of congeners and increases alcohol content. However, with each distillation you will remove more of the flavor and aroma compounds (remember, these are congeners), resulting in a product closer and closer to neutral spirits (vodka) with each run. If you are going to redistill your spirit, you should plan to do so in advance to make the most effective and efficient use of your time.

One option is simply to collect your heads, hearts, and tails from multiple batches and combine the like types together (e.g., combine only the heads from each batch) and redistill each when you have enough to reasonably run in your boiler. The advantage to this method is that you will get the most from each collection stage, and your hearts will become more refined and smoother. The disadvantage, of course, is that you must make multiple batches before you will have any finished, drinkable spirits.

Another method is to make your cuts somewhat less precise, starting your middle-run collection just slightly into the heads and continuing it slightly into the tails. You can then dilute the distillate that you have collected in the middle run to reduce the proof to below 80 (below 40%abv) and increase the volume to fill your boiler to at least 50 percent of its capacity. Never try to distill a product that is over 40%abv (80 proof)! The higher the alcohol percentage, the greater the risk of fire. If there is space in the boiler, add additional water to further reduce the proof while still leaving 20 percent open space in the kettle for expansion. The additional water will separate very efficiently from your alcohol due to the difference in their boiling points, so this will not adversely affect your finished product. You can then redistill the product, making more precise cuts. As you have already tossed the foreshots, you should not have any remaining in your second distillation.

Using a Thumper

This talk about redistilling is moot if you have a thumper, as you have already essentially double-distilled your spirit. This virtual second distillation helps separate some of the components that are boiling off at the same time from your pot distiller. However, you cannot make cuts based on temperature when using a thumper, so you must use your nose, taste buds, and alcoholmeter to help you along.

To set up your thumper, you will connect it directly to the output from your pot still. You must connect your thumper between your kettle and your condenser, as the thumper will only work if you supply it with vapor, not condensate. The vapor will be taken directly from the head of your pot still and be directed to the bottom of the thumper. You will generally fill the thumper approximately halfway with liquid, but depending on the size and shape of the thumper, you may need

to adjust the fill level. Assuming that the volume of your thumper is optimal for your distillation, a taller and more slender design is much more effective, as it gives the incoming vapor much more contact time with the cool liquid, allowing it the time needed to be condensed and exchange heat with the liquid in the thumper. If your thumper is too shallow, then the vapor may not get condensed, and it will not be effective.

Watching the temperature at the head of your distiller is still a good way to gauge where you are in the process, but remember that the vapor entering the thumper is being condensed, and just as it takes time for your distiller to come up to a temperature where it will begin producing vapor, so does your thumper. Be patient. It will take some time for the incoming vapor to heat your thumper liquid to the point that vapor will begin to be produced.

That brings us to another point. What is the best liquid to use in your thumper? If you have tails from a previous run available, that is your best option. This is because there is already a reasonable amount of alcohol in the solution, so as the liquid heats, you will expel that alcohol. If you choose to use the tails from a previous batch, it is best to use only the tails that are collected earliest to reduce the concentration of fusel oils and other tails congeners. Your second-best option is to use some of the wash that you are going to distill, as there is alcohol present, albeit far less than in tails from a previous run. Water is your last resort, and given that you have the wash already on hand, there is really no reason to use water in your thumper.

Just as you would with a pot distillation, always collect in small containers, such as glass pint jars, marking them according to when they were collected through the run. Toss the first 4 ounces (125ml) as your foreshots. Smell and taste each container to decide which jars should be included in your finished spirit and which should be held aside for a subsequent distillation.

Reflux Distillation

While with pot distilling we are trying to pull a specific range of components from the wash, including flavor and aroma compounds in addition to our alcohol, with reflux distillation we are generally after pure alcohol. That is not to say that reflux distillation cannot be used to produce fantastic flavored spirits. In fact, more and more people are turning to reflux distillation as a way to gain greater control over what fractions they collect, making it possible to collect only specific flavor and aroma compounds along with the alcohol. This is because careful control of a well-designed reflux distiller will give very distinct separation of the compounds in the wash. For our purposes here, we will be focusing on reflux distillation for the collection of pure ethanol.

A reflux distiller with sight glasses on the column.

Before we go any further, it is important to point out that no matter how carefully and precisely you control your distiller, and no matter how wonderful the design is or how slowly you try to run it, you will not be able to achieve 100 percent alcohol. Although pure ethanol boils at 173° F (78.3° C) and water boils at 212° F (100° C), a mixture of 95 percent ethanol and 5 percent water actually boils at a lower temperature than either of these compounds, boiling at 172.7° F (78.15° C). The mixture of 95 percent ethanol and 5 percent water therefore cannot be separated by distillation. This is known as an azeotrope. Through very precise control, it is sometimes possible to "jump" the azeotrope, achieving up to 95.6%abv (191.2 proof). To increase the alcohol percentage further requires a process called drying. Drying is simply a matter of removing the extra water from the alcohol. However, it is not a simple process. Generally, the drying of alcohol requires use of molecular sieve material, which is a special material that absorbs water but does not absorb the alcohol, thus pulling the water from the alcohol and leaving it at or near 100 percent. The primary reason to dry the alcohol is if you intend to use the alcohol as a fuel, such as for a car, lawnmower, tractor, etc. Ethanol as a fuel is used in sports such as racing and is the "85" in E85 fuel. The problem with 95 percent ethanol and 5 percent water is that, when combined with gasoline, the water may separate from the fuel, resulting in water in your gas tank. This is not a good situation.

An important thing to remember here is that you are not going to drink the alcohol at 100%abv. In fact, you will not drink it at 95%abv, or 90%abv. While striving to purify the alcohol as much as possible through reflux distillation has obvious foundation—that is, removing the maximum amount of congeners, resulting in the cleanest, most neutral product possible—further drying is of no value in beverage alcohol, as you will be diluting the product to a drinkable strength anyway. For the purpose of distilling neutral beverage alcohol, we will strive for the highest purity possible, and for that we will use reflux distillation. Because our goal is to produce a neutral product, what you choose to ferment will have little bearing on the final result. However, if you ferment a strongly flavored wash, such as a grape wine, then it will be more difficult to achieve the clean, neutral product that you seek. With that said, your finished product will never be completely neutral. If neutral spirits such as vodka were truly neutral, then all vodkas would taste the same. More accurately, they would not taste like anything at all. But if you have ever tasted vodka you know that there are good vodkas and bad vodkas, but they all carry trace characters that differentiate them. While you will not taste the base grain, fruit, etc., what was used in the fermentation will definitely affect the final product, as different materials tend to produce slightly different congeners. Although in many circles it is felt that the best vodkas are made from a wheat malt mash, there are also many perfectly acceptable vodkas made from corn, rye, potato, and even dextrose (corn sugar) and simple granulated sugar. I highly suggest that your first steps into the hobby are with a simple sugar wash and turbo yeast, using reflux distillation. This will ease you into the hobby with the least number of potential mistakes and help you build a comfort level with basic fermentation and distillation. Many people never move beyond this point. There is nothing wrong with that. This is a hobby with many interest levels and many different ways to ferment and distill.

The first steps in reflux distillation are the same as that for pot distillation, so there is no point in elaborating on them.

Step 1: Ferment and clear your wash

Step 2: Transfer the wash to your kettle.

Now things will change up a little.

Step 3: Assemble your distiller. This will include inserting the column packing material into your distillation column and attaching it to the kettle. If you have not already done so, wash your column packing and rinse it very well. The bit of residual water is not of concern.

If you are using a loose fill, such as ceramic raschig rings, you will want to assemble your distillation column with a screen at the bottom of the column to hold the column filling in place. Lean the column at about a 45 degree angle and pour in the rings until your column is filled to within 1 to 2 inches of where the condenser attaches to the column. Do not fill the column above this point, as you do not want to potentially block the vapor's access to the condenser!

If you are using copper mesh column packing, cut pieces to an appropriate length, depending on the weight of the copper "thread" and the size of your distillation column. For a 2-inch column, most copper mesh can be cut to approximately 4 feet in length, and for a 3-inch column, you will likely need 10 to 12 feet. Lay the copper on a counter and loosely roll it along the width of the mesh, resulting in a mesh "plug" that is approximately 6 inches wide and the inside

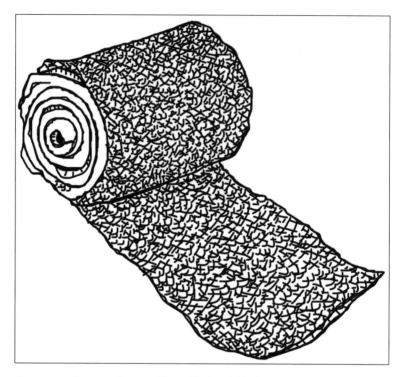

diameter of your column. The roll should be large enough to grip the wall of the distillation column so that it is held in place by friction, but not so large that you need to compress it substantially to get it into the column. Doing so can restrict the amount of space available for the rising vapors and refluxing liquid, resulting in a situation called choking. Choking occurs when there is not enough open space for both the rising vapor and falling liquid, and a "wall" will be created with liquid on one side and vapor on the other. No vapor will be rising to the top of the column, so distillation will cease and the temperature will fall. However, the boiling liquid continues to produce more vapor, creating pressure below the wall. The pressure will continue to build until the vapor bursts through. This will be seen as a sudden surge of liquid from the condenser and a spike in the temperature at the head of the column. The column resets, and the process starts all over. This can often be corrected by reducing the input heat, which in turn reduces the speed at which vapor is produced but will also reduce your distillation speed, often dramatically.

Step 4: Start heating the still. Now that your still is assembled, you can start heating it. A stable heat source is extremely important in reflux distillation. While it is certainly beneficial in pot distillation to have a consistent heat source, in reflux distillation, it is absolutely necessary. If the level of heat that you apply to the boiler changes, so does the speed at which vapor is produced. For the degree of separation of compounds that you are relying on to achieve the highly purified alcohol at the top of the column, you must give the column a consistent flow of vapor. If vapor production increases, then all the fractions get pushed a little bit further up the column. You are then forced to adjust your flow of cooling water at the top of the column to control this increased amount of vapor. If vapor production then decreases, all the fractions move closer to the bottom of the column, and you may not have any vapor reaching the top of the column at all. A consistent heat source, and one that does not cycle on and off (as many hotplates do), will save you a lot of grief.

Step 5: Start running your cooling water. You will have a little bit more time before needing to start running your cooling water when you are running a reflux column, because not only does the liquid have to come to a boil, but the rising vapor must heat all the packing material and the distillation column itself. As the vapor rises, it will give much of its heat to the distillation column and packing, resulting in the vapor cooling and condensing. Already you are using the height of the distillation column to work for you. As the process progresses, you will be able to literally feel how high the vapor has reached by touching the column but be careful, as it is extremely hot! It is neat to see how precisely layered the heat is. You can literally be touching cold metal, and less than an inch lower is so hot that you instantly pull your hand away. This is where the excitement and anticipation really start to take over, as you can visualize what is taking place inside the column and you become anxious for what comes next. Once you are able to feel the heat begin to rise in the column, it is a good idea to start the cooling water. This process will start very slowly and then proceed more quickly as the vapors rise further in the column, so you must be very attentive at this point.

Depending on your column design, you may wish to hold the column in "full reflux" for a short time after the vapor reaches the top of the column prior to the condenser or takeoff point. Full reflux simply means that all the vapor is being refluxed, or condensed and falling back down the column, and nothing is being collected. The idea behind this is that it give your column additional time to "set up," separating the fractions more precisely. If you have a distillation column that is very tall in relation to the diameter, then a very good degree of separation will occur naturally as the vapor rises and heats the column and packing material. This is especially true of reflux columns with cooling tubes through the column that are placed just slightly below the connection for the condenser, as these cooling lines will force an extra level of reflux before any vapor is able to exit.

Step 6: Remove the foreshots. Just as with pot distillation, the temperature at the head of the column will remain roughly the same as the ambient air temperature until vapor reaches the top of the column. At that point, the reading on the thermometer will rise almost instantly to the vapor temperature, which will usually be around 148.5° F (65° F)—the boiling point of methanol. Within a few seconds, drops of clear liquid will start slowly emerging from your condenser. You may notice that the temperature will continue to rise, but much more slowly after reaching this temperature. This is because there is generally very little methanol to be removed, and given the degree of separation in your reflux column, you will quickly exhaust the methanol and will be removing other congeners with boiling points below that of ethanol. Because of the relatively higher level of separation taking place in reflux distillation, you can generally discard far less of the first distillate as foreshots. While discarding the first 1 to 1.25 ounces (30-40ml) is generally considered sufficient in reflux distillation, I highly suggest opting for a slightly larger amount (just as in pot distillation), closer to 3 ounces (90ml). The few pennies lost will prove to be well spent when you taste your final product.

Step 7: Start collecting your distillate. Your column should be settling into a nice, steady pace now. The temperature should have risen to approximately 172° F (78° C) and should hopefully be holding

steady. Distillate should be dripping from your condenser at a medium
to fast drip, but not a trickle (except for very large columns). Unlike
with pot distillation, there will be no need to monitor the temperature
to separate heads, hearts, or tails if you have equilibrium in your column and do not try to push the column beyond its capabilities. With a
carefully run reflux column, the by-products comprising the foreshots
and heads will be concentrated into the first 3 to 4 ounces (90ml to
120ml), and you will not begin to collect tails until virtually all of the
alcohol has been collected. At that point, you will simply move to the
next step. This means do not try to distill too quickly! Patience is a vir-
tue, and it will pay dividends in reflux distillation. Remember that pot
distillation is performing a single distillation, whereas reflux distillation is essentially performing the work of several distillations in one
run. This means that while you will be getting much more separation
and purity from your reflux distillation, it will be markedly slower. Do
not try to rush the process by turning up the heat. For most hobby-
size reflux stills, you will not be able to collect more than 1 quart (most
2-inch-diameter columns) to 2 quarts (most 3-inch-diameter columns) of distillate per hour. Yes, that may sound very slow, and watching the *drip drip drip*, while exciting at first, quickly leaves you wanting
to speed up the process. Doing so will result in a substantial decrease
in the quality of your distillate. You will definitely be rewarded for your
patience.

If you are using a parrot, your alcoholmeter should hopefully be
showing a very high percentage of alcohol in your distillate, at least
90%abv and hopefully closer to 93%abv to 95%abv. If you do not have
a parrot, then start collecting your distillate into your test cylinder and
test it with your alcoholmeter. This distillate may still smell "raw,"
and if you want to taste it, do so only by getting a drop onto your finger. Never try drinking such potent alcohol without first diluting it!
Providing your input heat and your cooling water temperature remain
constant, then the temperature at the head of the column, your distillate flow, and the proof of the distillate should also remain stable. This
will continue for several hours, depending on the volume of alcohol in
your wash and the size of your column.

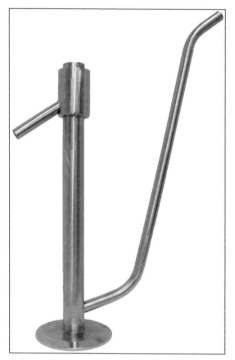

Step 8: Calling it quits—when to stop collecting. As the time continues to pass and your thermometer appears to be almost stuck on a certain temperature, you will begin to wonder if this will ever end. What started out as a fun project is suddenly feeling very boring. Admittedly, there is not much fun in watching the constant dripping from the condenser, nor in checking the thermometer only to find that exactly nothing has changed. Consider this a good thing. If you ever experience a constantly fluctuating temperature at the head of the column or surging from the condenser and at some point you most likely will—then you will suddenly gain a new appreciation for the boring, stable temperature reading.

So how do you know when it is time to stop collecting and shut down the still? If your distiller has a very well-balanced match between heat input and cooling, and a well-designed reflux column, then often you will notice a marked decline in the speed at which your distillate is being produced. The dripping of spirit from the condenser will become slower, although the proof will remain above 90%abv. The production rate will continue to slow, you will glance at how much distillate you have already collected, and decide that enough is enough. Often a quick calculation of the amount of alcohol collected versus the amount that was in the kettle when you started will show that you have collected nearly all the available alcohol already. If it does not appear that you have collected nearly all the available alcohol that you started with, then you may need to increase your heat input or reduce your cooling, although that is usually obvious far earlier in the process. Sure, you can continue to collect until either distillate stops being produced or a rise in the temperature at the head of the still shows that you have moved on to higher alcohols and fusel oils, but why? Distillate is likely being produced so slowly at this point that it is not worth the cost of heating the still anymore. This is a good time to shut down the distiller and call it a good day.

The other scenario is that you will see the temperature at the head of the still increase. Just as noted above, this means that you are moving into tails, which can be collected and added to your next batch to ensure that there is no lost alcohol. However, in most cases there is so little alcohol remaining at this point that it is usually not worth the cost to continue heating the distiller to collect the small amount of alcohol.

Step 9: Shutting down the distiller. Turn off the heat. do not turn off the cooling water! As discussed previously, just because you have turned off the heat does not mean that there is no vapor being produced. The liquid remaining in the kettle is still very hot and well above 173° F (78.3° F)—the boiling point of ethanol. That means that if there is any ethanol remaining in the kettle, it will continue to rise into the column. Keep the cooling water to both the column and the condenser running until you are certain that there is no more vapor rising to the top of the column. Because you have stopped heating the distiller and are continuing to run the cooling water to the column, you will likely see an immediate and dramatic drop in the temperature at the head of the still. Once the temperature has dropped to well below 173° F (78.3° F), you should remove the thermometer from the top of your still head or loosen the still head to allow adequate airflow back into the distiller to avoid the possibility of imploding your distiller. As soon as the kettle is cool enough to handle, dump the liquid remaining in your kettle. Wash and rinse your distiller as per the manufacturer's recommendations.

Step 10: Cutting and storing. Unlike with pot distillation, most reflux distillation is done to achieve a more neutral spirit, such as vodka. Obviously, outside of use as a fuel, your alcohol will not be used at the high proof that you have collected it at. While it can be stored in glass containers at this high proof, it is best to reduce the proof of the spirit for safety. The higher that the proof of the spirit is, the more flammable it is. If you are after the cleanest, most neutral spirit possible, then you will want to carbon filter the spirit, which cannot be done effectively at the high proof you have collected. This is another reason to reduce the proof of the spirit at this point.

Gin Still

The gin still is used to infuse flavor and aroma into your spirit. By building a gin basket (the container that holds the herbs, seeds, etc.) into a reflux column, directly before the collection point (where the condenser collects), you can eliminate the need for a second "infusion" distillation while achieving the same results. In this two-step process, you first distill your spirits, then dilute them and redistill in a pot distiller that has the infusion material suspended above the boiling liquid. The alcohol vapors will pass through the gin basket, picking up flavor and aroma from the material in it. This distillate is then carried to the condenser and into your collection container. On forced reflux columns that employ a system such as the internal cooling tubes below the condenser connection, you can eliminate the need for a second step by installing the gin basket between the cooling lines and the condenser. In this design, the highly purified vapor is forced to flow through the material in the gin basket, picking up flavor and aroma compounds on its way to the condenser.

The distillation process is virtually identical to that used for reflux distillation, simply with the addition of the gin basket for added flavor and aroma.

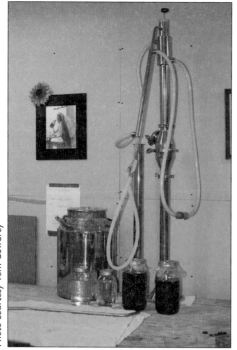

Photo courtesy Tom Cowdrey

Gin still, assembled, on propane heater.

Countertop Distiller

Available under several brand names, this distiller is simply a modified water distiller that is more adept at alcohol distillation than the original version. Generally, the modifications that have been made to the distiller are to replace the standard heating element with a lower wattage version, extend the condenser (increase condensing capability), and close the chlorine relief valve (to reduce the risk of alcohol vapor entering the air). These systems are extremely simple to use and are entirely self-contained, so there is no additional heat source or cooling water required. You simply add your wash up to the fill line, install the lid, and plug the unit in. They are a pot distiller of sorts, but there is no thermometer to test the vapor temperature, and because of the small volume (most of these units only distill about a gallon of wash at one time), it is nearly impossible to make cuts based on the alcohol percentage. It is still possible to successfully distill flavored spirits by collecting in very small containers and using taste and smell, but these distillers are best used for distilling more neutral spirits. The majority of these distillers have a 4-liter capacity, so all directions are based on this volume. If you have a larger or smaller version, then you will need to adjust your volumes accordingly.

Photo courtesy Megahome

This type of distiller is also still capable of distilling water, although it will do so at a slower pace than an unmodified version due to the reduced wattage heating element. The primary difference between distilling water and alcohol using this type of distiller is that you will allow the unit to distill until it is entirely dry when distilling water. When distilling alcohol with the modified countertop distiller, you must manually stop the distillation process by unplugging the distiller once a predetermined amount of distillate has been collected. You will usually collect roughly one-third of the original volume of wash in the distiller, and this product will usually be a little more than double the proof of the wash. You should discard the first ounce (30ml) of distillate as foreshots.

If you are attempting to distill neutral spirits, then you can collect the next 1.4 liters as usable spirits. Alternatively, you can collect only 1 liter as usable spirits and collect the subsequent liter in a separate container for redistillation. By collecting only 1 liter, you will have a cleaner spirit with fewer congeners and a higher alcohol content. The next liter of distillate can be collected as tails and will have a reduced alcohol content, but more congeners. You can hold this second liter of distillate aside in a sealed glass container and combine it with the tails from other batches to be redistilled into a much cleaner spirit. This method, while requiring slightly more effort, will reduce the loss of usable alcohol and greatly improve the finished product.

Because this is a pot-distilled spirit, it is highly advisable to filter the spirits through activated carbon to remove many of the congeners in the distillate.

Calculating the Available Alcohol and Collected Alcohol

All of this talk about calculating how much alcohol you had available and how much you have collected is not very helpful if you do not know how to calculate these things. First, we will calculate how much alcohol was available when you transferred your wash into the kettle. This is why taking specific gravity readings is very important. Without them, you are just guessing, and that will not work well in these calculations. Second, we will calculate how much alcohol we have collected. If you have collected a very high percentage of the original alcohol, then it is usually most economical to simply call it quits. If you have not collected a high percentage of the available alcohol, then you need to consider the possible causes and adjust your procedure accordingly.

To calculate the percentage of alcohol by volume (%abv) transferred into your kettle, subtract your final specific gravity from your original specific gravity and multiply that number by 131.25. For example, if your original specific gravity was 1.095 and your final specific gravity was 0.990, then your percent alcohol by volume is 13.8 percent. Multiply this number by the volume of wash that you transfer to your kettle to find the volume of alcohol available.

Original SG 1.095

- Final SG   0.990

Difference   0.105

0.105 x 131.25 =13.78%abv

For 5 gallons of wash;

abv 0.1378 5 gallons (18.9L) = 0.689 gallons of alcohol (2.60L of alcohol)

As you can see, for the sake of gaining a more usable number, it is usually best to use liters for your volume and not gallons. To gain an accurate figure, you must be as accurate as possible in all of your readings, including the actual volume of wash that you place in your kettle.

Calculating the amount of alcohol that you have collected is a very simple procedure. Simply take the volume of distillate and multiply it by the percentage of alcohol by volume. For example, if you collect 2.5 liters of distillate at 95%abv, then you have collected 2.375 liters of alcohol.

Collected: 2.5L x abv 0.95 = 2.375

In this example, you would have collected just over 90 percent of the available alcohol. It is common to collect closer to 95 percent or more, even without collecting into the tails.

Temperature Variation

You have probably noticed by this point that I refer to very precise temperatures for making cuts and especially the temperature that you should expect to see at the head of your distillation column when you are operating a reflux distiller. This may not exactly match the thermometer reading at the top of your column, however, and this can be extremely concerning if you do not understand the reasons for this variation. The two primary causes are the elevation at which you are distilling and the thermometer itself.

Elevation likely has the greatest effect on the boiling point of a liquid. The boiling points referenced above are those for specific compounds at sea level. As your elevation increases, the boiling point of all liquids, including ethanol, decreases. Similarly, if you are located below sea level, then the boiling point increases. This means that if you are distilling at 3,000 feet above sea level, the boiling point of alcohol will be reduced by approximately 5° F, or 3° C, to approximately 168° F (75.5° C). As little as just a few hundred feet above sea level will result in a noticeable decrease in the boiling point. Since most people live at least somewhat above sea level, it is common to reach an optimal head temperature below 173° F (78.3° C). The actual reason for the change in boiling point with respect to elevation is that the atmospheric pressure is lower as elevation increases. As a result, you can even have a slight increase or decrease in the boiling point based on the weather, as the atmospheric pressure changes along with it.

Another cause of an unexpected temperature reading is the inaccuracy of the specific thermometer that you are using. Most thermometers supplied with hobby distillers in fact, most thermometers not specifically designed for extremely accurate readings will have a certain variance in their accuracy. In other words, your thermometer is likely not something that you would want to rely on in an extremely sensitive situation. Many hobby-grade thermometers have a 1 percent accuracy, or nearly 2° F (1° C) accuracy at our standard operating temperatures.

Thermometer placement is a less common cause of unexpected temperature readings. Generally, this happens when the bulb of the thermometer is placed too low in the column and you are reading a different vapor than what is actually reaching your condenser, or you are too near the reflux cooling (especially in the case of internal cooling lines), resulting in a lower reading than expected.

Thermometer Placement

This leads us to another point—what is the best placement for the thermometer? If you have spent much time researching distillers on the Internet, you have surely seen many designs and thermometer locations both at the top of the distillation column as well as in the kettle. Ultimately, your primary concern is the temperature of the vapor that exits the column to the condenser, which is then condensed and collected. Therefore, the optimal place for your thermometer is at the top of your column. This is how you are able to decide whether or not you wish to collect the distillate that is exiting the condenser.

Why, then, do some distillers have a thermometer placed in the kettle? Often this placement of a thermometer gives the appearance of offering valuable information. Providing there is also a thermometer placed at the top of the column, then the placement of a thermometer in the kettle is not actually hurting anything. However, there are a few systems that have a thermometer only in the kettle, and this will leave you running blind with respect to the temperature at the head of the column.

Based on the placement of the thermometer in the kettle, there are essentially two temperatures that you can read. First is the temperature of the liquid, and second is the temperature of the vapor being produced. Reading the temperature of the liquid will only tell you that your liquid is in fact heating or that it has reached its boiling point. This information is of very little value. Touching your hand to the side of the kettle will confirm that the heat you are supplying is in fact heating the liquid. Knowing that the majority of the wash is a combination of water and alcohol, and knowing what percentage of each is in the wash, you can generally calculate its boiling point. What this reading will tell you, however, is approximately how much alcohol is remaining in the wash. As the boiling point of the liquid nears the boiling point of water, you will know that most of the alcohol has been removed. Of course, knowing how much alcohol was available in the first place, and looking at how much you have collected, you can estimate this same information, often more accurately and far more easily.

Reading the vapor temperature in the kettle is not of significantly more value. There has been no substantial separation of compounds this near to the boiling liquid, so the vapor temperature will not be dramatically different.

To Strip or Not to Strip

No, this does not involve a pole and dollar bills. A "stripping run" is simply a fast distillation of the wash without concern for making cuts, collecting all the distillate until the output drops to around 20%abv. The resulting distillate is known as low wines. You then re-distill the low wines as you normally would for the specific type of produce, either by pot distillation or reflux distillation.

The idea behind this process is that you will remove water and some of the harsher higher alcohols, leaving you in a position for an easier second distillation with a cleaner finished product. This is probably one of the more adamantly defended practices in distillation, with strong opinions on both sides. Many insist that the stripping run dramatically improves the product collected on the subsequent distillation, while others suggest that a slightly slower and more precise single distillation is just as effective, with considerably less time and energy cost spent on a slower single distillation. Because opinions run so strongly, it is best to try both methods and make your own decision.

Cool Down: Getting Rid of the Backset as Quickly as Possible

While we have listed the basic steps of safely shutting down the distiller once you have collected all the distillate, we have not yet discussed why it's so important to get the hot liquid out of your kettle as quickly as possible. The fermented wash is very acidic, and the backset is potentially even more so. Most distiller boilers are made of either copper or stainless steel, and both are easily corroded by the acidic wash. Allowing the wash to cool by sitting overnight may sound like the best alternative, as it is obviously much safer to handle cooled liquid than while it is still hot enough to scald you, it is not a good alternative from the kettle's point of view. So even if you are not saving the backset for future use, getting it out of the kettle as quickly as is safely reasonable to do so will help ensure a longer life for your kettle.

A Note about Diluting

The spirit coming from straight out of your distiller is generally too potent to be consumed directly. This is especially true of reflux distillation, in which you often distill in excess of 90% abv alcohol. Such a high proof is not only unpleasant, but also unsafe to drink. If for any reason you want to taste this strength of spirit, just touch your finger to the spirit and then to your tongue. Never try to drink high-proof spirits! There is simply no reason ever to do otherwise.

Reducing the proof of the spirit to a level where it can be safely consumed is one of the reasons to dilute the spirit with water. Another reason is safety when storing the spirit. While 90 to 95%abv ethanol can make a great solvent, it is also extremely flammable. Reducing the proof for storage is a much safer alternative. If you intend to store any of your spirit at a high proof to use for cleaning, it is best to store it with your other poisonous and flammable items, such as paint thinner.

Diluting the spirit is simply a matter of mixing the alcohol with water. However, simply using tap water for dilution may result in a mixture that suddenly turns into an unappealing, cloudy product. The primary cause of this issue is based on certain minerals that may exist in your water. These minerals are soluble in water but are not soluble in alcohol, so when the minerals in your water are introduced to the alcohol, they immediately come out of solution, turning the spirit cloudy. The minerals will settle to the bottom of your container over time, or they can be filtered out of solution with a very fine filter, such as a wine filter. However, it is far simpler to just avoid this potential pitfall in the first place by using demineralized water. Any water with a very low mineral count is usually acceptable.

Most distilled and reverse osmosis bottled water has a very low mineral count, but be careful, as some of these bottled waters have minerals added to them to give the water some character. Most bottled spring water will have a much higher mineral count, so it can be unacceptable for diluting your product. If purchasing bottled water to dilute your spirits, check the mineral count and opt for the lowest possible, usually under 10 parts per mmillion (ppm). Another option is to simply distill your own water. After all, you have a distiller, and water distillation is a simple and relatively quick process compared to alcohol distillation.

The calculation to dilute your spirit to a certain finished strength is rather straightforward. There are multiple different calculations available, but I find that it is handled most easily by using a three-step calculation. First, you calculate the amount of ethanol contained in your distillate. You then calculate the total volume of product that this spirit will produce at your desired %abv. The difference between the total finished volume and the volume of distillate that you are starting with is the amount of water that you need to add. As with many of the calculations, it is easiest to use liters or quarts as your system of measure, as percentages of a gallon can be more difficult to compute accurately.

For example, if you are starting with 2 liters of distillate at 90%abv, and you would like to store this distillate at 50%abv, then you will add 1.6 liters of water to the distillate, giving you 3.6 liters of diluted spirits at 50%abv.

2L x 0.90 = 1.8L (this is the volume of ethanol in your undiluted distillate)

1.8L ÷ 0.50 = 3.6L (this is the finished volume of distillate that will be produced)

3.6L - 2L = 1.6L (this is the amount of water required to dilute your spirit)

5. Filtering Your Spirits

Why We Filter Spirits

FILTERING YOUR SPIRITS, also known as polishing, is a process in which you remove congeners remaining in the spirit even after distillation. It is used almost exclusively in the production of neutral spirits (vodka) and is most commonly done by running the distilled spirits through activated carbon. Filtering flavored spirits would be counterproductive, as it would strip out all the flavor and aroma compounds that you have worked so hard to achieve. However, in the case of vodka, the less character the better, so we filter the spirits to remove as many of these trace congeners as possible.

Unfortunately, filtration is a step that is often skipped by many hobby distillers. They feel that their spirit is clean enough, and for them it may be. Their friends say that it is the best vodka that they have ever tasted, but remember these are their friends, and this is free alcohol. Very few people are critical of free alcohol. If you want the cleanest product possible, and one that your friends will truly feel is the best that they have ever tasted, then you absolutely must filter your spirits.

But you have fermented a wash destined to become the cleanest, purest product that you have ever tasted, making sure to use the most appropriate yeast and that it had adequate nutrition and little stress. You took the utmost care in distilling that wash, exercising great patience despite the overwhelming desire to speed the process up. You took all the precautions to make sure that your spirit is safe to drink, and it smells clean enough. So why would you need to filter your spirit? Quite simply, your spirit is not as clean as you think, and you will not fully appreciate this until you have filtered it. Only then will you realize just how much better your spirits can be and how many congeners were in the spirit needing to be removed to have a truly neutral product.

What is activated carbon?

Contrary to what many people believe, activated carbon is not charcoal. Several terms are thrown around by people who are referring to the same thing, but in reality they are thinking of entirely different products. The most commonly misused terms that people use when they mean to refer to activated carbon are carbon and charcoal. Carbon is actually a chemical element, found on the periodic table. Charcoal is essentially a porous form of carbon that is the result of burning a product, such as wood, in the absence of air. This may sound like nitpicking, but to avoid confusion and ensure that you have the correct product for filtering your spirits, it is important that the correct term be used. Some flavored spirits, most notably some whiskies, are actually filtered through charred wood. This filtering will not strip a substantial amount of flavor, but it does pull out some of the more harsh congeners, resulting in a smoother product that still contains the desired flavor. If this same product was filtered through activated carbon, it would strip most of the character and flavor, resulting in a very upset head distiller. Hopefully you now understand the importance of using the correct term, and if in any doubt, clarifying what you are referring to so that you obtain the correct product. Activated charcoal is another term that is often used when referring to activated carbon, but this term is technically correct. Note that the key word in all of this is the word "activated." Activated carbon is produced from many different products through a combination of carbonization and chemical activation to create a carbon with many tiny pores of different sizes.

There are literally hundreds of types of activated carbon available, of which only a few are suitable for the filtering of spirits. It should go without saying that you should use only food-grade activated carbon. There are many types of activated carbon that are not intended for use in human food applications, so do not assume that all activated carbon is human food grade. Beyond simply being food-grade, there are other factors that affect the ability of any given activated carbon to strip congeners from your spirit, resulting in a clean, neutral product. Choosing an inappropriate activated carbon will not simply be less effective, but it can actually reduce the quality of your spirits by leaching deposits from the carbon that will end up in your finished product.

The type of material that the activated carbon is manufactured from, along with the exact activation method, will result in an activated carbon with different pore structures. Not all activated carbon is suitable for alcohol filtration, or even liquid filtration, for that matter. The optimal end use for the activated carbon depends greatly on the pore structure within the grains of carbon, as well as the format of the carbon. The basic formats for activated carbon are powdered, pelletized, and granular. Powdered carbon is not a usable format for most liquid filtration as it will quickly pack, forming a mud-like product that will not allow liquid to pass through it in a manner that is conducive to spirit filtration. Pelletized carbon, which is formed using powdered carbon under high pressure, is often used in water filtration (e.g., fish aquariums), where the water will be continuously circulated through the carbon or otherwise has an extended contact time with the carbon. It does not offer a large surface area or provide good access to the carbon pores when using standard spirit filtration methods. While both powdered and pelletized activated carbon have many uses, neither of these types is suitable for alcohol filtration.

Now you know that you are limited to granular-activated carbon, but there are still many types to choose from. So how do you know which is best? Ultimately, the "best" carbon depends on exactly what is to be removed from the liquid and how you intend to go about the filtering process. What we do know is that a larger percentage of the molecules that we wish to remove from our spirit measure between 2 nanmeters and 10 nanometers in size. These molecules will become trapped in the pores of the carbon, which is a process known as adsorption (not to be confused with absorption). This brings us back to the pore structure of the activated carbon. To trap these molecules, we will need to have an appropriate pore structure in the carbon. There are three types of pores created in the carbon during the activation process: macro pores (larger than 25nm), meso pores (1nm to 25nm), and micro pores (smaller than 1nm). Given the size of the molecules that we need to trap, the macro pores will have little effect on our spirit, as most of the compounds can flow right through without becoming trapped. At the opposite end of the spectrum are micro pores, which are too small to allow most of the compounds to even enter the pore. Meso pores, on the other hand, are of great value. The percentage of each pore type within the activated carbon is controlled by the selection of base material used and the activation process employed in making the activated carbon.

The two methods of making activated carbon are chemical activation and steam activation. Because most chemically activated carbon is wood-based and usually ground into powdered form, it need not be discussed at length. Steam activation is employed for most of the materials that are used in spirit filtration. The most common materials used for activated carbon intended for alcohol filtration are peat, stone coal, and coconut shell.

Peat-based activated carbon has primarily micro pores and meso pores, making it ideal for alcohol filtration. Unfortunately, it is difficult to obtain for the average hobby distiller, and because it is a relatively soft form of activated carbon, it does not hold up well to regeneration (the cleaning of activated carbon for reuse).

Stone coal–based activated carbon is similar to peat-based activated carbon in that it has a high percentage of micro pores and meso pores. This type of activated carbon is much more widely available than peat-based activated carbon and comes in a variety of grain sizes. Being a much harder carbon it is also better suited for regeneration, which can reduce the cost by allowing use of the same carbon multiple times.

Coconut shell–based activated carbon contains almost exclusively micro pores, but it can be extremely effective in alcohol filtration because the extremely large number of micro pores in the carbon can trap molecules at the entrance to the pores. This is only effective with very slow filtration, but it can make coconut shell–activated carbon among the best choices for alcohol filtration as a result. Coconut shell–activated carbon is also a physically hard carbon, making it suitable for regeneration.

Grain size is another consideration that you must give thought to when selecting your activated carbon. Grain size is often expressed either as mesh size range (e.g., 20x40) or the physical size of the granules (e.g., 0.4mm to 0.85mm). Both of these refer to the same thing, that being the size of the carbon granules. Mesh size refers to the size of the openings in a mesh screen. For example, No. 20 mesh has openings that are approximately 0.841mm in size, and No. 40 mesh has openings of approximately 0.42mm. This means that all particles 0.841mm and smaller are able to pass through the No. 20 screen, while larger particles are unable to pass through it. If the particles that pass through the No. 20 mesh are further separated using a No. 40 mesh, then all particles 0.42mm in size and smaller will pass through the screen. The granules that passed through the No. 20 mesh but could not pass through the No. 40 mesh will therefore fall between roughly 0.42mm and 0.84mm. Figures for this carbon are usually rounded to 0.4mm to 0.85mm when describing the granule size. The common mesh/granule sizes used in spirit filtration are 20x40 (0.4 to 0.85mm) and 14x40 (0.4 to 1.4mm). Most wood or peat carbon are of smaller granule size, commonly 18x60 (0.25 to 1mm).

Although the size of the grain does not affect the pore structure, it does affect how we must go about filtering to get the best possible results from filtration. A larger grain size, such as 0.4mm to 1.4mm versus 0.4 to 0.85, can do an excellent job of filtering and is more suitable for in-home regeneration, where the granules may get broken into smaller pieces. However, filtration must be done more slowly to be highly effective. Generally a smaller grain size will allow for faster filtration, but as the size of the activated carbon decreases, you can increase the risk of the filter becoming clogged, just as you will with powdered carbon. 0.4mm to 0.85mm (20x40 mesh) is a good middle ground, where the risk of the filter becoming blocked is minimal, speed of filtration is good, and it is widely accessible inexpensively.

Cleaning the Carbon

Once food-grade carbon has been activated, it is acid washed and then rinsed with water to remove water soluble minerals remaining in the carbon. It is not uncommon for the carbon to be poorly rinsed, especially with activated carbon made from base materials such as coconut shell, which can be more difficult to rinse. This can result in a deposit remaining in the activated carbon that will end up in your filtered product if the carbon is not properly rinsed prior to use. This is best done using a two-step process: first soaking the activated carbon in water, followed by rinsing.

These instructions are for a standard hobby-size package of carbon (approximately 104in³, 1.7L). If you are using a different volume of carbon, you should adjust all measurements accordingly.

Start by putting your dry activated carbon into a large container, such as a mixing bowl. Be sure to allow room for a few quarts of water to be added to the bowl along with the carbon. Bring approximately three quarts (about 3L) of water to a simmer and pour the water into the bowl. Stir the carbon gently and allow it to rest for a few minutes. You will likely notice an oily film on top of the water. Once the carbon has settled, pour the water off the carbon, being careful not to pour the carbon out with the water. Repeat this process at least three to four more times. This process will clean much of the deposit from the carbon while also saturating the activated carbon with water. By fully saturating the carbon, you will improve the efficiency of the filtration, as more of the distillate will be forced through the carbon instead of simply running around the carbon granules.

You can further improve the saturation and resulting efficiency by adding simmering water after your final rinse and allowing it to sit undisturbed for 24 hours.

Although it is not necessary to follow the entire rinsing procedure with properly regenerated carbon, it is still necessary to add simmering water and allow the carbon to become saturated prior to the filtration process. Failing to do this will dramatically reduce the efficiency and effectiveness of the activated carbon filtration.

Secondary rinsing is done as part of the startup process for the spirit filtration, as outlined below.

Alcohol Filtration

The most effective method for activated carbon filtration is the one that allows you to force the maximum amount of liquid through the pores in the carbon so that the largest number of contaminants are trapped inside the granules of carbon. As discussed, activated carbon does not use ionic charge to remove contaminants. Activated carbon works by trapping molecules within the carbon itself, so to be effective, we must find a way to force the liquid through the carbon as opposed to just channeling it around the grains of carbon. Wetting the carbon during the rinsing process lays the groundwork, but we still must employ a method that encourages the liquid to channel through the carbon and not around it. Always remember that most particles are lazy, so they will take the path of least resistance as they make their way through your filter system. That path is usually around the carbon, unless you set up your activated carbon bed appropriately. This is precisely why tossing carbon into a container with your spirits will do very little. While a small amount of spirit will flow through the carbon's pores this way, the overwhelming percentage will not. Most of the spirit is quite happy to just flow around the granules of carbon as they settle to the bottom of the container. You may hear that shaking the container regularly to rouse the carbon will help. Indeed, each time the carbon settles, some of the liquid will flow through the carbon instead of around it. However, what about the liquid that flows through the pores in the opposite direction from the previous time? It can dislodge molecules that were previously trapped in the carbon, releasing them back into the spirit. To use activated carbon to efficiently and effectively remove the residual flavor and aroma compounds remaining in the spirit after distillation, you must force the maximum amount of liquid through the carbon so that the congeners are trapped and removed from your product. The best way to do this is by creating a long filter bed that maximizes the liquid's contact with the activated carbon.

Another consideration that we must take into account is the proof of the spirit that you will filter. In most cases, if you attempt to filter undiluted spirit, say 90%abv or more, your filtration attempt will prove unsuccessful. The high-proof spirit has a lower density, and as a result this thinner consistency liquid will usually channel around the carbon granules, resulting in negligible improvement. To ensure consistent, effective results, you should dilute your spirits to no more than 55%abv prior to filtration. While you can dilute your distillate further, there is no reason to do so at this point, as it simply increases the volume of liquid, and therefore the time involved to filter. You can further dilute your filtered spirits to the desired proof later. This also allows for the small amount of dilution that will take place during the filtration process.

To obtain the maximum contact time and liquid interaction with the activated carbon, it is best to employ a long, narrow tube that you will fill with your activated carbon. This creates the greatest likelihood of spirit flowing through the pores of the carbon, where the contaminants will be trapped. The result is the cleanest possible finished product.

In commercial distilleries, it is common to use a pump to pump the spirit up the column as opposed to using gravity to feed the distillate. This allows a greater level of control over the speed of flow, as well as being optimal for steam regeneration, as pressurized steam can be fed from the top of the filter column, forcing many of

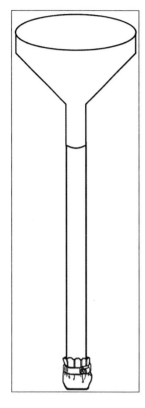

the contaminants in the carbon out of the pores, vaporizing them, and carrying them out to a drain. This is not economically feasible in a hobby-level activated carbon filter system. Instead, we use a gravity feed system and try to regulate the flow rate either by the number of filter papers used (to control resistance) or with a valve on the output.

A basic activated carbon filter system is both simple and inexpensive to build. There are also several commercial filter systems available, ranging from low-cost plastic systems to high-end stainless-steel filters. If building or purchasing a plastic filter system, be sure to use only food-grade, alcohol-tolerant parts. The most common types of tubing for hobby distillation filtering systems are PVC and ABS. If given the option, you should select ABS plastic, as it is more tolerant to ethanol than is PVC. This is important even at the reduced strength involved during filtration.

Shape and size of the filter is of paramount concern. A square filter—or any filter shape with distinct corners—creates far too many void spaces that are not filled by the carbon. As a result, the spirit will channel through these void areas and not be forced through the carbon, or even between the grains of carbon. If the filter is too narrow, then the spirit will often channel down the walls of the filter, bypassing almost all interaction with the activated carbon. In both instances, the result is that there will be no substantial improvement to your spirits. Always opt for a round tube with a minimum inside diameter of 1.5 inches (40mm). An optimal volume of activated carbon for two to three gallons of spirit (a common volume of 50%abv spirit resulting from a six-gallon distillation) is around 100 to 110in^3 (1.6 to 1.8L). To obtain this volume using a

1.5-inch-inside-diameter tube, you will need the length to be approximately 60 inches:

Volume = $\pi r^2 h$

Volume = $3.14159 \times 0.75^{"2} \times 60"$

Volume = $106 in^3$

Using a larger-diameter filter tube will allow you to reduce the length of the tube in relation, as it will still provide the same amount of contact time with the carbon. Similar to distillation, increasing the diameter of your filter column can allow for an increase in the speed of filtration, but only if the overall volume of activated carbon being used increases accordingly. This is how commercial distilleries are able to filter a large volume of spirits relatively quickly. Just as with distillation, patience will pay off, as filtration is far more effective when done

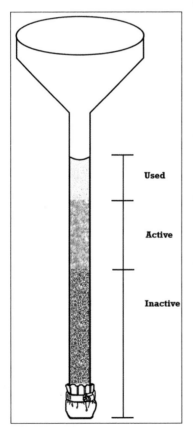

slowly. A good filtration speed using a $105 in^3$ carbon filter is 1 quart (946ml) per hour, although up to 2 quarts (1.89L) per hour is generally very effective.

Building your own carbon filter is very simple and cost-effective. You already know that a 1.5-inch (40mm) tube that is 60 inches (1.5m) long will act as a very effective filter tube. As luck would have it, 1.5-inch food-grade PVC tubing is available at virtually all home building supply stores and for just a few dollars.

On top of the filter, you need some form of reservoir, unless you are willing to stand beside the filter and constantly add your unfiltered spirit. I didn't think so. A great, low-cost option is a large, food-grade plastic funnel. You may find a suitable funnel at a department store, but in all likelihood you will need to go to your local homebrew store for this item. There is no magical perfect size, but the larger your funnel, the less often you will have to check on it or top it up. Next you will need some way to seal the funnel to your filter tube. If the connection between the funnel and filter tube is not sealed, then liquid will seep out through the connection. There are many options for this step, from silicone gaskets to permanently connecting the two parts with food-grade adhesive.

You now have a filter tube with reservoir, but you still need something to hold the activated carbon inside the filter tube, control flow rate, and filter the tiny particles of carbon from the filtered spirits. All three of these tasks can be handled by affixing filter paper(s) to the bottom of the filter tube. This is most easily done by wrapping the filter paper(s) around the bottom of the tube and holding them tightly in place with a large stainless-steel hose clamp. The number of filter papers to use will depend on the type of filter paper that you have selected. While two to three commercial filter papers will usually be sufficient, if you decide to use coffee filter papers, you will require considerably more to avoid tearing and to decrease the speed of filtration. Now you just need to decide how you will suspend the filter above your collection container (hint, standing the filter in a colander that is situated above your collection container works very well).

Congratulations! Your filter system is built and ready to use.

The filtration of spirits is considered by many people to be a slow process, but it does not need to be annoying or a hassle. You have already prepared your activated carbon, and your filter system is built and ready to go. Filtration, unlike distillation, is not a process that you need to be constantly present for. Providing you remember to top up your reservoir before it is completely empty, this can be a relatively painless but very worthwhile process.

It is now time to move your wet carbon into the filter. Because the wet carbon tends to fall down the tube in heavy clumps, it is best to support the bottom of the tube by balancing it on a solid surface to avoid tearing the papers. Add approximately 1 pint (473ml) to the filter tube to slow the descent of the carbon and help build a consistent filter bed. Begin transferring your carbon to the filter using a serving spoon or ladle. After each addition, tap the side of the filter tube lightly to reduce gaps in the carbon. Once all the carbon has been added to your filter you can start the secondary rinsing, followed by the spirit filtration.

The secondary rinsing serves two purposes. First, it rinses away the last of the deposits in the carbon that may not have been removed during the previous rinsing and wetting procedure. Second, it helps to reduce any air gaps between the carbon granules, which reduces the channeling of liquid around the carbon and maximizes the flow through the carbon. To perform this step add approximately one gallon (3.78L) of hot water to the reservoir. The reason to use hot water will be evident in a moment.

When the water in the reservoir has nearly disappeared below the top of the carbon, start adding your unfiltered spirits. DO NOT LET THE WATER OR SPIRIT LEVEL DROP BELOW THE TOP OF THE CARBON! Doing so will allow air to enter into the system and require you to reset your filter by running at least a gallon of water through the system to rid it of air. Always start adding your spirits before the water has completely drained from the reservoir. Yes, this will result in a very small amount of dilution, but that is to be expected during the filtration process and is one of the reasons to filter at a higher proof than is meant for consumption. There will not be any dilution in the filter column, as both the water and spirit are moving down the tube at the same rate of speed.

Collect the liquid that is dripping from the filter, keeping a second container ready to start collecting your spirits separately when they begin to emerge. This is the reason for starting the filter using hot water. Your spirits will be cool—likely around room temperature—so by touching the filter column you will be able to actually feel where the water and alcohol are located as they move down the filter tube. When the alcohol has nearly reached the bottom of the filter tube, change your collection container to begin collecting your filtered spirits. Discard the water in the other container. Feel free to smell and taste the filtered product and note the difference between it and your unfiltered distillate. There should be a marked reduction in smell, flavor, and even the amount of "burn" on the tongue.

Continue adding your spirit to the filter reservoir. When the last of your unfiltered spirits have been added to the reservoir, it is time to start preparing for the final stage of filtration by heating a gallon (3.78L) of water. Just as you started adding spirits to your reservoir just before the last of the prep water disappeared below the top of the activated carbon, add the hot water to the reservoir before your alcohol has disappeared from sight. This water will help to push the alcohol through the system, leaving primarily water in the spent carbon and not wasting your valuable spirits. You can again feel on the filter tube where the alcohol and hot water meet as they progress down the filter column. Once the water has reached the bottom of the filter, you should replace the collection container with another container. Your alcohol is now ready to be further diluted and aged, flavored, or used as it is.

How to Know If Your Carbon Has Reached Its Capacity

As molecules become trapped in the pores of the carbon, they also begin to block those pores, rendering that portion of the carbon unusable. At the start of filtration, the carbon near the top of the filter will be actively removing the contaminants, and as it becomes used to its full capacity, the active area of filtration will slowly move down the filter column. The pores will gradually all become blocked by molecules that have been trapped, and the only way for the liquid to flow is by channeling around the carbon. When all the carbon has been used to its capacity, any further spirit will simply pass through the system unfiltered. The goal, especially for those who do not regenerate their carbon (which is the vast majority of home distillers), is to utilize the carbon to its full capacity without going beyond that point and simply passing their spirits through the filter needlessly. This is the most economical use of the carbon. Unfortunately, there is no magic number for gallons of spirit to volume of activated carbon. The purity of the distillate (i.e., how many congeners remain after distillation), the type of carbon selected, the filtration process, and the speed of filtration all play vital roles in this equation. As a rough rule of thumb, you can expect to effectively filter two to four gallons (7.56 to 15.1L) of relatively clean distilled spirit at 50%abv through 100in³ of good quality, appropriately selected activated carbon.

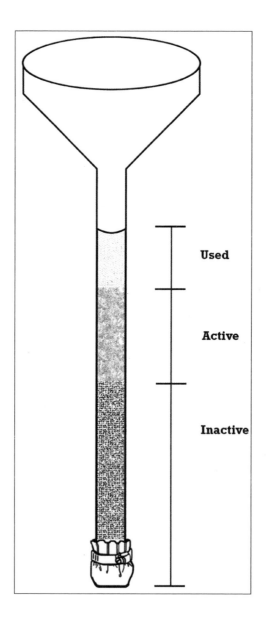

Regenerating Your Carbon

Once you have used the carbon you may choose to discard it, or you may decide to regenerate the carbon so that you can reuse it for future filtrations. Commercially activated carbon is most often regenerated and used many times, but this is far less common among hobbyists. This is in great part because of the cost factor of activated carbon. Commercial distilleries have to be far more concerned with cost than the hobby distiller. That is not to say that cost is not of concern to hobbyists, but they are not driven by cost the way that a for-profit distillery is. By regenerating and reusing their activated carbon many times, a distillery is able to make the activated carbon cost negligible. So why is this process less common among hobby distillers? Simply put, regeneration can be a hassle on a small scale. Commercial distilleries will put up the capital cost to be able to regenerate the carbon, knowing that it will dramatically reduce the cost impact versus replacing the carbon once it has been used. It is certainly feasible to build the same type of equipment on a small scale, but the cost is not justified unless volume is substantial. It is difficult for the hobbyist to justify spending a few hundred dollars just to enable him or her to regenerate the activated carbon that costs under $10 per batch, but much easier for a commercial distillery to justify a cost of a few thousand dollars for the same purpose given that they will reuse the same carbon up to 100 times or more.

With that said, it is not entirely unreasonable for the hobby distiller to regenerate activated carbon for at least a second or third use. The reason that commercial distilleries are able to reuse their carbon so many times while the hobbyist is much more limited is because of the way that the carbon is regenerated. While the distillery will use steam to regenerate the carbon, the hobby distiller generally must employ a combination of boiling and drying. The process can be a hassle and also dangerous if proper care is not taken. This is why most hobby distillers simply discard the used carbon and buy new carbon for each batch.

Note: Regenerating your carbon can be dangerous! Many of the contaminants in the carbon are extremely flammable. Never attempt to regenerate activated carbon with a gas stove or oven. Always have a fan running to disperse the air to dilute the flammable vapors and keep a fire extinguisher handy. Never leave the carbon unattended. These instructions are for informational purposes only. Regenerating activated carbon is not suggested and is done at your own risk.

If you decide that you are going to reuse your carbon, you will start by emptying the carbon from your filter column into a mesh sieve. Using a standard kitchen colander will not work, as the holes are larger than the carbon granules and they will simply flow through and down the drain. Rinse the carbon extremely well with hot tap water. Next, place the carbon in a large pot on the stove and add at least twice the amount of liquid. Bring the water to a boil and allow it to continue to boil for a minimum of 15 minutes. You will literally smell the contaminants that are being removed. Continue to boil until there is no longer a noticeable smell in the vapor. The boiling process breaks the carbon down slightly, so the granules will generally be slightly smaller after boiling. This is the main reason why the carbon can only be reused once or twice. As the carbon breaks into smaller pieces with each boiling, it quickly becomes too small to be used in a carbon filter tube without causing a blockage in the flow of the liquid.

At this point you have removed most of the contaminants with a boiling point of 212° F (100° C) or less. However, there are still fusel oils with a higher boiling point that remain in the carbon. To remove the remainder of the contaminants you need to dry the carbon in an electric oven. Never attempt to dry the carbon in a gas oven, as some of the contaminants remaining in the carbon are highly flammable and can ignite in a gas oven. Heat the oven to 300° F (150° C). Place the carbon on a cookie sheet or other shallow baking pan and allow to regenerate for approximately three hours.

It is important not to rush the process by increasing the temperature of the oven. Most of the impurities remaining after boiling have a vaporization point below 285° F (140° F), but as the temperature in the oven increases, so does the possibility of vapors (or even the carbon itself) igniting, so never exceed 300° F (150° C) when regenerating your activated carbon.

6. Aging and Flavoring

Adding the Finishing Touch

UNLESS YOU ARE using your filtered spirits as vodka, then you are not done just yet. It is true that vodka is the most popular of the different distilled spirits, but it is still only one of many. Whether you have just completed distilling a barley wash destined to become the next great whiskey, or the full depth and character of your brandy is just waiting to be captured, there is one final step necessary to realize the full potential of what your latest spirit can become. That step may be aging in an oak barrel for months, or even years, or it may be flavoring your spirit with fruit or even a commercial flavoring. At this point, the sky is the limit, and what you choose to do at this step can make an unbelievable difference in the product that finally makes it to your bottle.

First, we should separate into the two rather distinct groups—aging and flavoring. While you do certainly enhance and alter the flavors during the aging process, when we use the term "flavoring" we are referring to the intentional addition of specific flavors, such as is fruit or natural extracts, not the flavors that are contributed by aging in an oak barrel, for example. This is not to say that one method is better than the other. In fact, many commercial spirits are made by flavoring neutral spirits instead of by pot distilling a secret mash recipe and aging the distilled spirit. Commercially, it is all about consistency. The consumer expects the product that they purchase today to be exactly the same as the bottle that they purchased six months ago. That is often most easily attained with the addition of flavoring essences. However,

many will argue that this does not offer the depth of character that can be achieved by carefully crafting a recipe, distilling with accurate cuts, and then aging the spirit to bring out the subtle nuances and complexity. Whether this is true or not is always up for debate, and ultimately, it is probably as much a matter of individual taste preferences as actual differences in character.

One thing that is certain is that there are requirements, both legally and conceptually, that regulate what makes up each group of spirits. For example, rum is made from sugar cane, most often molasses, while whiskey is made from grain, most notably corn, barley, and rye. Whiskey is then further broken down into many different categories, such as Scotch whiskey, Irish whiskey, bourbon, etc. One thing that nearly all whiskies are known for is the character derived from aging in oak barrels. In fact, many spirits achieve at least part of their character from aging in wooden barrels, so that is where we will start.

Aging in Barrels

No, I did not specify oak barrels. This was intentional. While oak is the overwhelming winner, other types of wood are sometimes used to craft aging barrels. The type of wood selected will have a bearing on the final character, as the pore structure will be different, as will the actual flavor compounds that can be extracted from the wood. Even among oak barrels, you will generally have to select the type of oak. The most common options are American, French, and Hungarian. From these, you will need to select whether the inside of the barrel is charred (literally burned) or toasted (heated until the wood begins to darken), and even the level of charring or toasting. Each option contributes slightly different characteristics to the final product. This is where the complexity of many commercial whiskies comes from. They often employ multiple types of barrels at different stages in the aging process to capture characteristics from more than one type of barrel. This is not generally reasonable for hobby distillers, who will select a single oak barrel for the aging process.

An entire book could probably be devoted to the differences between the types of oak, region or forest that the wood was derived from, level of toasting or charring, conditions of storage, and a host of other variables. For the hobbyist, it really breaks down into a few basic considerations.

How to Select Your Barrel

Type of wood: American oak tends to contribute a slightly stronger flavor and aroma to the spirit than French oak, which is more subtle. This may lead you to select American oak over French oak, but a stronger flavor is not necessarily the best flavor. This is a matter of personal preference. Hungarian oak is very similar in character to French oak, but at considerably lower cost. Also note that when we are discussing aging any type of wine or spirits in oak, we are referring to white oak. Red oak is primarily used for furniture production.

Charred or toasted: In general, toasted barrels are used primarily for wine, while charred barrels are used for spirits. While this is often regulated for commercial spirits, the hobbyist is not under the same requirements and can select a barrel based on the desired character. The level of toasting or charring is based on how long the oak barrel is exposed to fire, starting with a light toast and progressing to a heavy char, often referred to as "alligator char" because the surface of the wood cracks, creating an appearance reminiscent of an alligator's skin. As the wood is heated, the sugars in the wood will caramelize and different levels of vanillins and tannins will develop. The carbon created by charring the wood will remove some of the harsh congeners in the spirit, which is why a spirit aged in a charred barrel tends to be much smoother in character than a spirit that has not been aged.

Size of barrel: The hobby distiller is not interested in the large barrels used by commercial distilleries. These are far too large for the small batches that the hobbyist produces. Instead, the hobby distiller will usually select barrels that are a few gallons in size or smaller. Common sizes available to the hobbyist range from 1/4 gallon (approximately 1L) to 5 gallons (19 to 20L). It is important to select a barrel that you will be able to fill completely, so do not simply opt for a larger barrel because it seems to be a better deal (small barrels can cost nearly as much as larger barrels). Aging will generally progress much more quickly in a smaller barrel than in a larger barrel and also much more quickly the first time that the barrel is used than on subsequent uses.

Barrel quality: Do not skimp on quality when you purchase a barrel for aging your spirits. If cost is a deciding factor, then it is far better to opt for one of the alternatives discussed later than to purchase a "cheap" barrel. Some low-cost barrels may utilize used furniture wood or a host of other tricks to be able to keep the price of the barrel down. They may also reduce the thickness of the barrel staves, shortening the life of the barrel and compromising its strength. Premium quality barrels are most often worth the difference in cost. You have come too far to risk the quality of your spirits now.

Curing the Barrel

No, your barrel is not sick, although it may have a bit of a leakage issue. When barrels are produced, the wood still has some moisture, the staves fit together very tightly, and the barrel does not leak if it is filled with liquid. When a barrel is in this state, it is called "tight." If the barrel is stored without liquid in it, as it often is between uses, then the wood will dry and gaps will form between the staves. At this point, if you add liquid to the barrel, it will run right out. Don't worry—in all but the worst cases your barrel is not ruined, it just needs to be tightened back up. This is actually a pretty simple process, but it varies slightly depending on whether or not your barrel is varnished or not. If your barrel has not been varnished, then you can simply fill a tub with water, remove the bung from the barrel, and submerge the barrel in the water. Depending on how dry the wood is, it can take anywhere from an hour or two to a day or more to fully tighten.

Tightening a varnished barrel can be done using the same procedure, but a water-based varnish will be destroyed using this method. Instead, remove the bung from the barrel, place the barrel in an open sink (no plug in the sink), and fill it with hot tap water. The water will leak out of the barrel and down the drain, avoiding a buildup of water around the outside of the barrel. Continually top up the barrel with hot water so that it continues to be absorbed by the wood. You should quickly see a reduction in the water draining from the barrel. When it appears that the barrel has stopped leaking entirely, fill the barrel completely, place the bung tightly into the bung hole, dry the outside of the barrel, and allow it to sit in the sink overnight to ensure that it is tight enough to hold your spirits.

Sterilizing Your Barrel

While this is not of substantial concern when aging distilled spirits because of the high proof involved, it is still good practice to keep all equipment clean and sanitized. Prior to use, you can burn a sulfur stick in the barrel (you can also use sulfur sticks as a way of keeping your barrel sterile during storage), ensuring that no spoilage organisms grow in the barrel. This is especially important for winemakers. However, the high-proof ethanol in your distilled spirit will sterilize the barrel. Before use, you should rinse the barrel extremely well with water to ensure that nothing is inside the barrel that should not be there. This includes mold that may have built up if the barrel was poorly stored. Once you are certain that the barrel is clean, then you can add some boiling water to the barrel. This will heat-sterilize the barrel. Let the water sit in the barrel for about five minutes, then drain it and add your spirits.

Barrel Alternatives

Often called "oak alternatives," the group of products used to replace wooden barrels are more accurately called "barrel alternatives," as many of these "alternatives" are in fact oak, just in a slightly different format. The most common options are chips, staves/sticks, cubes, and spirals. Aside from oak chips, all of the alternatives offer very similar benefits. So why would you want to use a barrel alternative instead of an actual barrel if both are made from the same wood? The answer is pretty simple—cost. A large part of the cost of a barrel is not the wood, but the tradesman (called a cooper) that actually makes the barrel. Therefore, you can purchase the wood at a much lower cost if it is not precisely cut, curved, and banded to become a barrel. So why would you purchase a barrel instead of the alternatives? There are a few answers to that question, including tradition and character. Tradition is self-explanatory. Character, however, may need further discussion, because it takes into account exactly what happens during the barrel-aging process.

When you age in a wooden barrel, there is some evaporation of alcohol and water through the pores of the wood and microscopic cracks between the staves. This loss is known as the "angels' share." This loss of volume is replaced by oxygen, which blends with the spirit in a form of micro-oxygenation. Aging with barrel alternatives is most often done in a sealed container, eliminating this exchange and oxygenation. The result is a slight difference in the final character between a barrel-aged product and one aged with barrel alternatives. There are several methods of controlling this on a commercial level, such as adding barrel alternatives to a barrel that has been used many times (the exchange of oxygen for evaporated spirit still takes place, while new oak is added to the barrel to obtain the character), or aging in stainless-steel drums with oak alternatives and controlling the oxygen levels in the drum. Obviously these are not feasible on a hobby scale.

One of the greatest advantages to barrel alternatives is the vast array of options available. Whereas your options for aging barrels are almost entirely within the oak family, barrel alternatives come in many different woods, including fruit woods such as apple, pecan, hickory, mesquite, and others. Each type of wood will lend a different character to the finished product, and you can even use a mixture of different types of wood to add more complexity and character to your spirits.

The format of the wood also has a slight bearing on the final character. Wood chips tend to be the lowest cost option, but have a distinct drawback in that they are all but impossible to char without destroying the wood entirely. This may be able to be offset somewhat by combining the charred chips with some toasted chips. Sticks, staves, cubes, and spirals all offer the advantage of being able to char the surface of the wood while leaving the underlying layers of the wood intact. This can give a character very close to that achieved by barrel aging, but at a fraction of the cost of a barrel.

How Much to Use

And that is the million dollar question. The problem is that there is no single answer to the question. The type of wood being used, the format of the wood, and a host of other variables will determine the final character derived through the aging process. As the surface area of the wood increases in relation to the volume of spirit being aged, the time required to achieve a given result decreases. That means that you will generally age more quickly in a small barrel than in a large one. You will age even more quickly if you use wood staves or cubes, and faster yet with wood chips. By increasing the amount of wood used, you will decrease the aging time as well. Of course, the character also varies, so it is a matter of balance. We all want to age our product as quickly as possible without compromising the quality or character of the finished product. This is probably even truer commercially, where storage space is at a premium and the longer it takes to get a product to market, the more the product costs. Fortunately, there is one method of cheating time, at least on a small scale, and to some degree.

Cheating Time

Part of the barrel-aging process comes from movement of the spirit in and out of the wood. As the temperature increases, the pores of the wood open and the spirit is brought into the wood. As the temperatures cool, the pores tighten, pushing the spirit back out. Think of the wood as a sponge. If you squeeze a wet sponge, the holes in the sponge close and the water runs out of it. When you release the sponge, the holes open and will suck water into them. You obviously cannot squeeze the wood hard enough to do this. However, you can still control this action by controlling the storage temperature. These changes in temperature happen naturally for large commercial producers that are storing their barrels in large warehouses. As the seasons change, so do the temperatures. On a small scale, you do have the ability to play Mother Nature. By moving your spirit into a cold area, such as a freezer, you have created winter. The pores on the wood will close and squeeze the spirit out. After a couple of weeks, it is springtime, and you can move your spirit to a warmer area, such as a closet or pantry. Repeating this a few times will have an astounding effect on your spirit.

This brings us to another question—how long should you age your spirits? Just as there is no right or wrong answer to how much wood to use, or even what type of wood or format, there is no perfect answer to how long you should age your spirit. The best way to achieve your desired result is by taking very small samples every week or two, and when you are satisfied with the taste, then it is time to remove it from the barrel/remove the wood from it, and bottle it.

With all of these variables, it may seem like I am avoiding specific answers to the questions that you have regarding aging your spirit. You wanted to know what the best method of aging was, what type of wood to use, how much, and for how long. Unfortunately, the only person who can answer those questions is you. Aging has a profound effect on your finished product, and all of these variables work together. However, there is one thing that can be answered specifically for you:

At what proof should your spirit be aged?

Aging proof: 124 (62%abv). Does that help make up for all of the perceived evasiveness in the previous information on aging? This number is not an arbitrary one that I simply pulled from thin air. It is shown to be the optimal proof to use when aging in wooden barrels (or with barrel alternatives, of course). At a range of 120 to 124 proof (60%abv to 62%abv) the alcohol can extract more of the desirable character from the wood. It also takes up less volume than aging at, say, 80 proof (40%abv), and storage space can be of concern to even hobby distillers. Increasing the proof beyond 124 can result in the extraction of harsh tannins from the wood, imparting a bitter, dry bite that is not considered a pleasant addition to most barrel-aged liquor. While a wee dram of cask strength may provide a nice warming effect on a cold evening, it is too strong for regular consumption, so you can further dilute to a more standard 80 proof (40%abv) prior to bottling.

Flavoring

I would bet that you are now more ready to hear about flavoring than you thought you would ever be. While you may have come off of the previous section thinking that aging in barrels or by adding oak chips or the like is far more complex than you had ever imagined, it is not. There is no arguing, however, that simply adding flavoring to your alcohol is a far easier process. It can provide a finished product that rivals traditionally aged spirits, and it does so in a fraction of the time and with far less fuss. So why has it not become the method of choice for virtually all hobby distillers and commercial distillers alike? Many feel that you cannot capture the subtle nuances of traditional aging with the simple addition of flavorings such as extracts and essences. However, flavor is just a combination of chemical compounds. No matter how complex one wants to make it out to be, virtually anything can be analyzed and replicated. Many of today's liquor essences have captured these characteristics surprisingly well. In one blind test, three out of five people picked the spirit made with vodka and essence to be the commercial product over the commercial product itself. That is not to say that they necessarily preferred it, but it at least shows how well some essences hit the mark.

Of course, there is no one brand that excels across the board, and all of the major brands have at least some flavors that they do particularly well. Not all essences are meant to replicate a specific commercial product, either. Many are a combination of commercial equivalents blended with the manufacturer's own personal taste preferences. The result is a selection of literally hundreds of options, and almost an infinite number of combinations created by you as the master blender.

One thing that does remain consistent among nearly all liquor essences is the manner in which they are used. The flavoring is added to your neutral spirit, sugar may be added to sweeten the product, and the product is bottled. Most styles of liquor produced using essence will improve over the first week or two as the flavors meld, creating a surprisingly complex and appealing product.

The addition of sugar noted above, and included in the instructions with many essences, has two effects on the finished spirit. The first effect is obvious—it sweetens the product. This is most often required as part of making liqueurs. The second effect is that a small amount of sugar can improve the body of the spirit. Even some commercial spirits will have a very small amount of sugar or glucose added just to improve the body of the finished product.

The first step in making liquor or liqueur with an essence is to calculate how much of your spirit is needed. To do this, we use the calculation previously mentioned for dilution. Assume that your spirit is stored at 50%abv, and you are making a 750ml bottle with a desired finished alcohol content of 30%abv. You will need 450ml of your spirit.

Desired: 750ml @ 30%abv

750 x 0.30 = 225ml (this is the amount of pure alcohol needed in 750ml to result in a 30%abv)

Now take the amount of pure alcohol needed and divide it by the percentage of alcohol in your existing spirits:

225ml ÷ 0.50 = 450ml

When adding sugar to your spirit, the simplest way to dissolve it is to place your alcohol and sugar in a blender and blend on high speed for 1 to 2 minutes. If making a cream liqueur, never add heavy cream to the blender, as you may end up with chunks of whipped cream, making a very unappealing product. Never try to dissolve sugar in alcohol that exceeds 140 proof (70%abv), as the sugar will not dissolve. Add the sweetened spirit to your bottle, along with the essence, and top up with de-mineralized water.

Of course, liquor essences are just one way of flavoring your spirit.

Alternate Methods of Flavoring Your Spirit

One alternative to flavoring using essences is to flavor using ingredients such as fruit. You can do this by simply soaking the fruit in the finished, filtered spirit and allowing the alcohol to absorb the flavor and aroma compounds and the color from the fruit. This method is best used for making liqueurs, as the alcohol will also absorb the fruit sugars, resulting in a somewhat sweet finished product. Some fruits that are especially well suited to this method of flavoring are peaches, many berries (strawberries, raspberries, blackberries, blueberries, etc.), and even apples. The quality of the fruit that you use will have a tremendous effect on the final product, so use only ripe, clean fruit that is free of visible damage. Cut the fruit to allow the alcohol to penetrate it, place in a glass jar, fill the jar with your spirit (80 to 100 proof is optimal), seal the jar, and set it aside. Give the jar a shake every few days. After about two weeks, open the jar and drain off the liquid, pressing the fruit to remove as much of the spirit as possible. Strain the spirit through a filter, such as a coffee filter, to remove any bits of fruit and solids, and bottle your liqueur. A great American-style schnapps can be made this way!

Another way to get flavor into your spirit is through infusion. Infusion takes us back to the distillation process and utilizes a gin column. However, instead of the host of ingredients used to make gin, you will suspend your choice of fruit or other material in the gin basket and allow the hot alcohol vapors to extract the flavor and aroma compounds from the material. The resulting product will be more like flavored vodka or German-style schnapps than the sweet product produced by soaking fruit in the distilled spirit.

Finally, remember that everything in this book is meant to guide you in the methods used to produce your own spirits as a hobby, but nothing can stop your imagination. After all, this is a hobby. Enjoy it. Do not be afraid to try new things, new recipes, or different methods. But always remember that you are dealing with flammable and potentially dangerous vapors, and exercise caution accordingly. This can be a fun and enjoyable hobby, and it even provides you with something to relax with at the end of your distilling day. Cheers!

A Final Note

Keeping records is one of the most important and often omitted steps in the entire distillation process. Without complete records, you nor anyone else can ever troubleshoot a problem that you may encounter at any stage in the process. Almost all brewers and distillers have had an issue at some point, whether it is a stuck fermentation or an unsuccessful filtration. Only when you are armed with the full recipe, specific gravity, temperature, etc., will you have the information to resolve the problem and avoid repeating it. Without records, you can also never expect to replicate your results, so when you sample your last batch and find it to be the finest spirit that you have ever tasted, you had better enjoy it while it lasts, as you will be unable to reproduce it. Maybe that last batch needs just a little change, but how much corn did you add again? You get the idea.

It takes only a moment to record the information for your batch. Keep records. At the very least, it can be fun sharing it with your friends as you sample your latest concoction.

PART ②

Distill at Home

7. Recipes

YOU MADE IT! It is finally time to start turning theory into practice and make some spirits and liqueurs. Remember that these recipes only touch on the vast number of variations, so feel free to change things up and experiment. In fact, I encourage it. That is how virtually every well-known brand came about. Home distilling is a fun and rewarding hobby, even if it does require keeping a low profile in most countries. So, without further adieu, let's get to making something!

Disclaimer: Having read up to this point, it is assumed that you know to fully clean and sanitize your equipment prior to use and how to use the fermentation equipment required to complete the process. It is therefore assumed that these steps do not require repeating in every recipe. The fact that they are not specified does not mean that they are not of utmost importance and a required part of the process.

Note: In all recipes, I will be suggesting the most appropriate yeast strain for the wash. By now you know the importance of using the correct yeast, and those suggested can be easily found at most homebrew supply stores that carry distillation supplies.

Vodka

We will start with a couple of recipes for vodka, as it is both the most popular spirit and the simplest to make. Originating in Russia, vodka is generally considered to be odorless, colorless, and flavorless. In other words, it is supposed to be as close to neutral in character as possible. Because vodka is supposed to be flavorless and therefore is not supposed to carry any flavors across during the distillation process, it does not matter what you ferment to make vodka. The control is in the distillation process. Vodka is generally distilled using a reflux method, as this allows for the purest spirit, although some vodkas are produced by distilling multiple times using pot distillation.

Because vodka is neutral, it is extremely versatile, which is likely the reason for its popularity. Being neutral in character also makes it ideal for flavoring, making it very useful in the production of other types of liquor and liqueurs. Both home distillers and some commercial distilleries will use vodka or NGS (neutral grain spirits) to produce products such as gin, whiskey, and rum, as well as liqueurs such as coffee liqueur, amaretto, and Irish cream. In fact, many home distillers are more than content staying with a simple sugar wash, which will be distilled to high purity, carbon filtered, and flavored using essence, and they may never venture out from there. This should not be frowned upon by those who wish to be more involved in the process. This is a hobby, and each person is limited by a different level of free time and interest. To start, we will repeat the simple sugar wash, followed by an all-grain vodka recipe.

Simple Sugar Wash

This is a basic recipe that should be almost everyone's first wash. The simplicity creates little risk for error, allowing you to focus on the distillation process. For those who do not have experience in home brewing or winemaking, this offers an easy entry into the fermentation process.

Ingredients:

14 pounds (6.3kg) granulated white sugar
6 US gallons (23L) of fresh, filtered or dechlorinated water
1 package of turbo yeast, sufficient for 6.6 US gallons (25L)
Clearing agent

Equipment required:

8-gallon or larger primary fermenter with tight-fitting lid
Airlock
Long-handled plastic spoon
Thermometer
Hydrometer
Test cylinder (optional)

Bring two gallons of water to a boil and add to fermenter. Dissolve sugar, adding more hot water if required. Top up fermenter with a combination of ice, cold water, or warm water to obtain a total volume of 6.6 US gallons (25L) at a starting temperature of 100° F (38°C) or other temperature as noted on turbo yeast package. Read and record the specific gravity using your hydrometer. Add turbo yeast and stir vigorously until all nutrients are dissolved and no clumps of yeast remain. Place lid and airlock on fermenter and allow to ferment in recommended temperature range until fermentation has completed. Read and record final specific gravity.

Once fermentation has completed, add the clearing agent as per package instructions. Once product has cleared, siphon to kettle and distill using reflux distillation.

Premium Grain Vodka

Although vodka is considered to be an odorless, colorless, and flavorless distilled spirit, in reality, some trace congeners will remain after distillation and filtration. Were this not the case, all vodkas would taste exactly the same, and you would not prefer one over another. Generally, those made from winter wheat are considered the finest quality, and is what many of the "ultra-premium" vodkas are made from. The recipe below uses a combination of malted wheat and flaked wheat. The malted wheat contains the enzymes necessary for converting the starches in the grain into fermentable sugars. Flaked wheat is wheat that has been run through hot rollers, which gelatinize the starches for rapid dispersion in the hot mash water. You can substitute the flaked wheat in the recipe with a different starch source, such as corn (another very popular grain used in the production of vodka, due to its low cost), potatoes, rice, etc., or a combination of these. Each variation will result in a slightly different character in your finished vodka, so experiment—what is generally considered to give the most favored may not be your own preference.

Ingredients:
2.2 pounds (1kg) wheat malt (crushed)
8.5 pounds (3.8kg) flaked wheat
1.5 teaspoon (7.5ml) gypsum
6 US gallons (23L) of fresh, filtered or dechlorinated water

Equipment required:
8- to 10-gallon stock pot with lid
8-gallon or larger primary fermenter with tight-fitting lid

1 package of vodka yeast with gluco-amylase enzyme, sufficient
for 6.6 US gallons (25L)

Airlock

Long-handled plastic spoon

Thermometer

Hydrometer

Test cylinder

Pour all of the water into your stock pot and heat until the water reaches 160° F (71°C). Stir in gypsum, then add flaked wheat and stir until grain has absorbed water and becomes soft and the mixture resembles oatmeal. If temperature is below 152° F (67° C), add heat to raise temperature to between 152° F (67° C) and 155° F (68° C), stirring mixture to avoid scorching. If temperature is above 155° F (68° C), allow mixture to cool until it reaches 155° F (68° C). Add wheat malt and stir gently to fully distribute grain. Place lid on the pot and allow it to rest for 60 to 90 minutes. Keep an eye on the temperature and stir gently every 10 to 15 minutes to ensure that the temperature remains between 149° F (65° C) and 155° F (68° C) during the entire mashing process. After 60 minutes, do an iodine test to check for completion of starch conversion. If starches are not completely converted, continue mashing process until an iodine test confirms that all starches have been converted.

Allow mash to rest until temperature falls to 90° F (32° C). Alternatively, you can rapidly cool the mash with a wort chiller, such as a copper coil with cold water circulating through it. Remove a sample of the liquid and take a hydrometer reading. The specific gravity (adjusted for temperature) should be in the range of 1.065.

Transfer mash to your fermenter. Pouring the mash, allowing it to splash into the fermenter, is a good way to help introduce oxygen into the mash. It is helpful to pour the mash back and forth several times and to stir vigorously to drive in as much oxygen as possible. Alternatively, you can use an aquarium pump and aeration stone in the wash for 30 to 60 minutes to fully aerate the mash.

Add the yeast as per package directions and allow wash to rest until fermentation has completed. Once fermentation has completed, strain the mash using a straining bag or other means of separating the solids from the liquid. The goal is to collect the maximum amount of liquid possible. You can even rinse the grain with a small amount of boiled and cooled water to maximize collection of the fermented liquid. Add the clearing agent per package directions and allow the wash to sit until cleared. Siphon the cleared liquid to your kettle and distill using reflux distillation.

Whiskey and Moonshine

Say what? What's the difference? Let's clear up the spelling concerns right now. Both "whisky" (without an "e") and "whiskey" are technically correct. There is no difference, except preference, which is often regional.

Whiskey really encompasses almost any flavored spirit made from grain. There are several types of whiskey, which are mostly distinguished by the type of grain that is used, but can also be dependent on the method of aging. For example, bourbon is a whiskey that is primarily made from corn. Scotch is, obviously, a whiskey of Scottish origin (and made entirely from barley), and rye whiskey is made using predominantly rye grain. Corn whiskey is actually distinguished from bourbon based on the percentage of corn used in the mash. Generally a minimum of 80 percent corn is required for corn whiskey versus a minimum of 51 percent corn for bourbon. There are some additional requirements from governing bodies (the Alcohol and Tobacco Tax and Trade Bureau, or TTB, in the United States) that must be met to use a given name to describe the spirit type. But as we are not dealing with spirits produced commercially, we will use the generally accepted terms to describe the spirits that we are making.

DME Whiskey

Named for the DME, or dried malt extract, that this recipe is based on, it is nearly as easy as the Simple Sugar Wash recipe used to make vodka.

Ingredients:

12 pounds light dried malt extract (note: 15 pounds of light liquid malt extract may be substituted)

6 gallons of fresh, filtered or dechlorinated water

1 package of whiskey yeast with gluco-amylase enzyme, sufficient for 6.6 US gallons (25L)

Clearing agent

Anti-foam agent

Equipment required:

8-gallon or larger primary fermenter with tight-fitting lid

Airlock

Long-handled plastic spoon

Thermometer

Hydrometer

Test cylinder (optional)

Bring two gallons of water to a boil and add to fermenter. Dissolve malt extract, adding more hot water if required. Top up fermenter with a combination of ice, cold water, or warm water to obtain a total volume of 6.6 US gallons (25L) at a starting temperature of 90° F (32° C) or other temperature as noted on turbo yeast package. Add yeast and stir vigorously until no clumps of yeast remain. Place lid and airlock on fermenter and allow to ferment in recommended temperature range until fermentation has completed.

Once fermentation has completed, add the clearing agent as per package instructions and allow the wash to clear. Do not confuse "clear" with "colorless." They are very different. The wash will retain color from the malt extract and will not become colorless. As the yeast settles to the bottom of the fermenter, the product will look much darker, but will be distinctly more clear. Once product has cleared, siphon to kettle, add the anti-foam agent as per package directions, and distill using pot distillation.

Scotch-Style Whiskey/Malt Whiskey

The recipe below will produce a nice smoky character Single Malt Scotch-style whiskey. You can increase or decrease the peated malt based on your preferences by substituting with the same amount of Golden Promise malt. You can also substitute the Golden Promise and peated malts entirely for a standard 2-row or 6-row malted barley to produce an American-style Malt Whiskey.

Ingredients:
9 pounds (4kg) Golden Promise malt (crushed)
1.5 pounds (.65kg) peated malt (crushed)
1.5 teaspoons (7.5ml) gypsum
6 US gallons (23L) of fresh, filtered or dechlorinated water

Equipment required:
8- to 10-gallon stock pot with lid
8-gallon or larger primary fermenter with tight-fitting lid
1 package of whiskey yeast with gluco-amylase enzyme, suffi-
    cient for 6.6 US gallons (25L)
Airlock
Long-handled plastic spoon
Thermometer
Hydrometer
Test cylinder

Pour all of the water into your stock pot and heat until the water reaches 160° F (71° C). Stir in gypsum, then add Golden Promise and peated malts and stir gently to evenly distribute grain. If temperature is below 152° F (67° C), add heat to raise temperature to between 152° F (67° C) and 155° F (68° C), stirring mixture to avoid scorching. If temperature is above 155° F (68° C), add ice or cold water to cool mash to 155° F (68° C). Place lid on the pot and allow it to rest for 60 to 90 minutes. Keep an eye on the temperature and stir gently every 10 to 15 minutes to ensure that the temperature remains between 149° F (65° C) and 155° F (68° C) during the entire mashing process. After 60 minutes, do an iodine test to check for completion of starch conversion. If starches are not completely converted, continue mashing process until an iodine test confirms that all starches have been converted.

Allow mash to rest until temperature falls to 90° F (32° C). Alternatively, you can rapidly cool the mash with a wort chiller, such as a copper coil with cold water circulating through it. Remove a sample of the liquid and take a hydrometer reading. The specific gravity (adjusted for temperature) should be in the range of 1.065.

Transfer mash to your fermenter. Pouring the mash, allowing it to splash into the fermenter, is a good way to help introduce oxygen into the mash. It is helpful to pour the mash back and forth several times and to stir vigorously to drive in as much oxygen as possible. Alternatively, you can use an aquarium pump and aeration stone in the wash for 30 to 60 minutes to fully aerate the mash.

Add the yeast as per package directions and allow wash to rest until fermentation has completed. Once fermentation has completed, strain the mash using a straining bag or other means of separating the solids from the liquid. The goal is to collect the maximum amount of liquid possible. You can even rinse the grain with a small amount of boiled and cooled water to maximize collection of the fermented liquid. Add the clearing agent per package directions and allow the wash to sit until cleared. Siphon the cleared liquid to your kettle and distill using pot distillation. If the distillate that you have collected is above 62%abv, then dilute to 62 percent and age in a charred oak barrel or with an alternative aging method, such as oak chips or oak staves.

Moonshine (a.k.a. No-Cook Mash)

While the term moonshine actually describes any illicitly distilled liquor, it is more commonly considered to be an unaged distilled spirit made from a primarily corn mash, making it fit nicely under the whiskey category for our purposes.

Ingredients:

8 pounds (4kg) flaked maize (in this recipe, you may substitute with cracked corn)
6 pounds (3.6kg) granulated sugar
1.5 teaspoons (7.5ml) gypsum
6 US gallons (23L) of fresh, filtered or de-chlorinated water

Equipment required:

8-gallon or larger primary fermenter with tight-fitting lid
1 package of whiskey yeast with gluco-amylase enzyme, sufficient for 6.6 US gallons (25L)
Airlock
Long-handled plastic spoon
Hydrometer
Test cylinder

Bring two gallons of water to a boil and dissolve sugar. Stir in gypsum. Pour mixture into fermenter and stir in flaked maize. Top up fermenter with warm or cool water to obtain a total volume of 6.6 US gallons (25L) at 90° F (32° C). Draw off a sample of the liquid and take a hydrometer test.

Add the yeast as per package directions and allow wash to rest until fermentation has completed (approximately three to five days). Once fermentation has completed, strain the mash using a straining bag or other means of separating the solids from the liquid. The goal is to collect the maximum amount of liquid possible. You can even rinse the grain with a small amount of boiled and cooled water to maximize collection of the fermented liquid. Add the clearing agent per package directions and allow the wash to sit until cleared. Siphon the cleared liquid to your kettle and distill using pot distillation.

Sour Mash

Sour mashing is a method in which a percentage of the fermented and boiled wash from a previous batch is added to a subsequent wash, usually at a minimum of 25 percent of the total wash volume. This means that in a 6.6 gallon (25L) wash you will use at least 1.65 gallons (6.25L) of "backset" in your new wash. The amount of backset that you use will have a distinct bearing on the character of the final product, so you can play with the volumes to get the flavor profile that you prefer.

While the sour mash method can be used with either a cooker-mash or a no-cook mash recipe, it is more common with no-cook recipes. The basics for each are outlined below.

Using the Sour Mash Method with a Cooker Mash

Ingredients:

2.2 pounds (1kg) 6-row pale malt (crushed)

8.5 pounds (3.8kg) flaked maize

1.5 teaspoons (7.5ml) gypsum

2 US gallons (7.5L) of backset (liquid remaining in boiler after distilling prior batch)

4 US gallons (15L) of fresh, filtered or dechlorinated water

Equipment required:

8- to 10-gallon stock pot with lid

8-gallon or larger primary fermenter with tight-fitting lid

1 package of whiskey yeast with gluco-amylase enzyme, sufficient for 6.6 US gallons (25L)

Airlock

Long-handled plastic spoon

Thermometer

Hydrometer

Test cylinder

Pour the backset and water into your stock pot and heat until it reaches 160° F (71° C). If this is your first batch and you therefore do not have any backset, then use 6 gallons (23L) of water. Without backset, this will not be a sour mash recipe, but you must start at some point. Add flaked maize and stir until the grain has absorbed water and becomes soft, and the mixture resembles the consistency of oatmeal. If temperature is below 152° F (67° C), add heat to raise temperature to between 152° F (67° C) and 155° F (68° C), stirring mixture to avoid scorching. If temperature is above 155° F (68° C), allow mixture to cool until it reaches 155° F (68° C). Add 6-row pale malt and stir gently to fully distribute grain. Place lid on the pot and allow it to rest for 60 to 90 minutes. Keep an eye on the temperature and stir gently every 10 to 15 minutes to ensure that the temperature remains between 149° F (65° C) and 155° F (68° C) during the entire mashing process. After 60 minutes, do an iodine test to check for completion of starch conversion. If starches are not completely converted, continue mashing process until an iodine test confirms that all starches have been converted.

Allow mash to rest until temperature falls to 90° F (32° C). Alternatively, you can rapidly cool the mash with a wort chiller, such as a copper coil with cold water circulating through it. Remove a sample of the liquid and take a hydrometer reading. The specific gravity (adjusted for temperature) should be in the range of 1.065.

Transfer mash to your fermenter. Pouring the mash, allowing it to splash into the fermenter, is a good way to help introduce oxygen into the mash. It is helpful to pour the mash back and forth several times and to stir vigorously to drive in as much oxygen as possible. Alternatively, you can use an aquarium pump and aeration stone in the wash for 30 to 60 minutes to fully aerate the mash.

Add the yeast as per package directions and allow wash to rest until fermentation has completed. Once fermentation has completed, strain the mash using a straining bag or other means of separating the solids from the liquid. The goal is to collect the maximum amount of liquid possible. Place lid and airlock on the fermenter and leave it to rest for 12 to 24 hours to allow any remaining solids to settle. Siphon the cleared liquid to your kettle and distill using pot distillation.

After you have completed the distillation, take two gallons of liquid from the boiler to use as backset for your next batch, following the same procedure above.

No-Cook Sour Mash Recipe

Ingredients:

8 pounds (4kg) flaked maize (in this recipe, you may substitute with cracked corn)

6 pounds (3.6kg) granulated sugar

1.5 teaspoons (7.5ml) gypsum

2 US gallons (7.5L) of backset from previous batch

4 US gallons (15L) of fresh, filtered or dechlorinated water

Equipment required:

8-gallon or larger primary fermenter with tight-fitting lid

1 package of whiskey yeast with gluco-amylase enzyme, sufficient for 6.6 US gallons (25L)

Airlock

Long-handled plastic spoon

Hydrometer

Test cylinder

Bring the backset to a boil and dissolve sugar. If this is your first batch and you do not have any backset, then replace the backset with 2 gallons of water. Stir in gypsum. Pour mixture into fermenter and stir in flaked maize. Top up fermenter with warm or cool water to obtain a total volume of 6.6 US Gallons (25L) at 90° F (32° C). Draw off a sample of the liquid and take a hydrometer test.

Add the yeast as per package directions and allow wash to rest until fermentation has completed (approximately three to five days).

Once fermentation has completed, strain the mash using a straining bag or other means of separating the solids from the liquid. The goal is to collect the maximum amount of liquid possible. Place lid and airlock on the fermenter and leave it to rest for 12 to 24 hours to allow any remaining solids to settle. Siphon the cleared liquid to your kettle and distill using pot distillation.

After you have completed the distillation, take two gallons of liquid from the boiler to use as backset for your next batch, repeating the procedure above.

Rum

Rum is a distilled spirit made from sugar cane or sugar cane by-products, most notably molasses. Due to the availability and subsequent low cost of sugar cane and sugar cane by-products, such as sugar cane syrup and molasses, rum is the most commonly produced spirit in Caribbean countries, and when one thinks of rum, they often associate it with its Caribbean roots. While there are certainly many styles of spirits that make up general categories such as whiskey or brandy, the range of flavor and character among the different styles of rum is much wider. The primary styles of rum are as follows:

White/light rum: These are the "raw" rum, if you will. While some countries require these rums to be aged, they are often filtered to remove most of the flavor and color gained by aging. In many countries, white rum is fermented, distilled, sometimes filtered, and immediately bottled and sold. As you can imagine, these rums have the least amount of character, although they will contain some character, therefore not qualifying them as vodka. Light rum is most often distilled in a column or reflux distiller.

Gold rum: Sometimes called "amber rum," these rums are, as the name implies, darker in color than light rums. The color and much of the character in a gold rum is achieved by aging the distilled rum in charred oak barrels. In addition to adding color, the barrel aging contributes flavor and aroma to the rum, as well as a smoothing or mellowing of the rum. Gold rum is often distilled in a column or reflux distiller, but may also be distilled in a pot distiller.

Dark rum: Generally aged for a longer period than gold rum, dark rum will pick up more color and character from the barrel-aging process. In addition, many dark rums will have a small amount of caramelized sugar dissolved in the rum, further adding to the deep color and sugar cane character. Dark rum carries a much stronger character and is often distilled in a pot distiller.

Spiced rum: As its name implies, spiced rum is a rum with the addition of different spices added, most commonly cinnamon, orange zest, cloves, allspice, and pepper. Spiced rums are most often based on gold rum.

The recipe for making rum is very basic—sugar cane juice/molasses, water, and the appropriate yeast. However, there are a couple of variations.

Molasses Rum

This produces the most flavorful rum, although it is also slightly higher in cost than the brown sugar method. Still, if you are going to go through the work to make rum, isn't it worth the slightly higher cost to produce a superior finished product?

Light Rum

Ingredients:
1 gallon sugar cane juice or light molasses
5 gallons water
1 package rum turbo yeast
1 package clearing agent
Anti-foam agent

Equipment required:
8-gallon or larger primary fermenter with tight-fitting lid
Airlock
Long-handled plastic spoon

Hydrometer

Test cylinder

Heat two gallons of water to 170° F (77° C) and add to fermenter. Dissolve molasses. Add three gallons of water to obtain a temperature of 90° F (32° C) or other temperature as specified on the yeast package. Stir vigorously or use an aeration stone to oxygenate the wash. Take hydrometer reading. Pitch yeast and stir until all nutrients are fully dissolved and no clumps of yeast remain. Allow to ferment within the temperature range noted on the yeast package until fermentation has completed, usually three to five days. Add clearing agent as per package directions and allow wash to clear. Siphon cleared liquid to boiler, add anti-foam agent, and distill in a reflux distiller. You can optionally carbon filter the rum, but this will leave the finished product more like vodka than rum.

Brown Sugar Rum

Brown sugar is simply white sugar with some molasses remaining, or in many cases, it is white sugar with some molasses added back to it. Therefore, brown sugar is capable of making a light-bodied rum. It will not make a full-flavored rum, as you are diluting your character by using what is essentially diluted molasses. However, it will produce a perfectly acceptable light rum for many people and is a lower cost wash to produce.

The procedure is identical to the recipe above, with the exception of the molasses. For brown sugar rum, you will substitute 15 pounds of brown sugar for the gallon of molasses. Once you have dissolved the brown sugar, you will follow the recipe exactly the same way.

Gold Rum or Dark Rum

The recipe for gold rum or dark rum is the same. How you distill and age determines the final type of rum that you will end up with.

Ingredients:

1 gallon sugar medium molasses

5 gallons water

1 package rum turbo yeast
1 package clearing agent
Anti-foam agent

Equipment required:
8-gallon or larger primary fermenter with tight-fitting lid
Airlock
Long-handled plastic spoon
Hydrometer
Test cylinder

Heat two gallons of water to 170° F (77° C) and add to fermenter. Dissolve molasses. Add three gallons of water to obtain a temperature of 90° F (32° C) or other temperature as specified on the yeast package. Stir vigorously or use an aeration stone to oxygenate the wash. Take hydrometer reading. Pitch yeast and stir until all nutrients are fully dissolved and no clumps of yeast remain. Allow to ferment within the temperature range noted on the yeast package until fermentation has completed, usually three to five days. Add clearing agent as per package directions and allow wash to clear.

For gold rum: Siphon cleared liquid to boiler, add anti-foam agent, and distill in a reflux distiller. Age the rum in a charred oak barrel or with oak alternatives (charred oak sticks, etc.) at 60 to 62%abv. Aging time will depend on the method of aging, so take small samples on a regular basis until you achieve the level of character that you prefer.

For dark rum: Siphon cleared liquid to boiler, add anti-foam agent, and distill in a pot distiller. Age the rum in a charred oak barrel or with oak alternatives (charred oak sticks, etc.) at 60 to 62%abv. Aging time will depend on the method of aging, so take small samples on a regular basis until you achieve the level of character that you prefer. Once aging is complete, add a small amount of caramelized sugar to the rum to add additional color and the slight sweetness and burnt sugar character reminiscent of Caribbean-style dark rums.

Spiced Rum

Spiced rum is made using an already completed rum, adding your spices, and allowing the rum to extract the flavors from them. The recipe below is for an individual bottle of spiced rum, which is a good volume to start with until you have found a recipe that suits your own tastes. Of course, it can be a fun journey finding just the right blend of spices!

Ingredients:

1 25-ounce (750ml) bottle of gold rum

1 vanilla bean (split lengthwise)

¾ cinnamon stick, broken into small pieces or ground

⅛ teaspoon fresh nutmeg (ground)

3 cloves

3 allspice berries

3 peppercorns (cracked)

1 star anise segment

2 tablespoons orange zest (orange peel with no pith)

Combine all ingredients in a 1-quart jar and seal. Shake mixture daily. Taste daily after two days until desired flavor has been reached. Strain rum through a coffee filter to remove all spices and sediment.

Brandy

Brandy is simply a fermented and distilled fruit juice. In other words, brandy is just distilled wine. When the term brandy is not further qualified (e.g., peach brandy), then it is generally considered a grape brandy. Brandy is usually distilled using a pot distillation method and then aged in charred oak barrels, where it will gain color and character from the oak.

The simplest option for making a brandy is to purchase an inexpensive winemaking kit and ferment as per the kit's directions (excluding adding any oak and stabilizer packages). This eliminates the need to crush and de-stem grapes or to find grape juice that does not contain any stabilizing agents, as these would inhibit fermentation, just as they are meant to do.

(Grape) Brandy

Ingredients:

6.5 gallons (25L) white grape juice (without stabilizers or preservatives) or frozen grape juice, mixed as per container directions to make 6.5 gallons

1 package pectic enzyme

1 package schnapps yeast

1 package clearing agent

Anti-foam agent

Equipment required:

8-gallon or larger primary fermenter with tight-fitting lid

Airlock

Long-handled plastic spoon

Hydrometer

Test cylinder

Pour grape juice into fermenter and stir in pectic enzyme. Take hydrometer reading. Add schnapps yeast and stir until all nutrients are dissolved and no clumps of yeast remain. Allow to ferment in the recommended temperature range until fermentation has completed (usually five to seven days). Add clearing agent and allow wash to clear. Siphon wash to boiler and add anti-foam agent. Distill using a pot distiller. Dilute distillate to 60 to 62%abv and age in charred oak barrel or with comparable alternative, such as charred oak staves, until desired character has been reached.

Fruit Brandy

To make a fruit brandy, you will follow the same recipe as for grape brandy, but you will replace the grape juice with another fruit juice. Peach, pear, and apple are among the most common fruit brandies.

Schnapps

Schnapps is a completely different product depending on where you are from. In Germany and much of Europe, schnapps is a strong, flavored, vodka-type beverage. It is made the same way that brandy is made, but the clear distillate that is collected is simply diluted to "consumption strength," which is usually around 40%abv (80 proof).

The American version of schnapps is more like a liqueur, which is often much heavier in fruit character, diluted to a lower alcohol level, and sweetened. They are generally made by taking a neutral spirit such as vodka and adding fruit or fruit flavoring. Obviously, the simplest option here is to purchase commercial liqueur essences, but in case you want to try your hand at making an American-style schnapps from scratch, I have included a recipe below.

Peach Schnapps

Ingredients:
5 ounces (450ml) 40%abv vodka
1 cup distilled water
1 cup sugar
2 large peaches

Slice peaches and place in a 2-quart canning jar. Bring water to a boil and dissolve sugar. Allow mixture to cool, then add vodka. Pour mixture over peaches and seal jar. Allow mixture to rest for two to three weeks or until desired flavor has been achieved. Filter liqueur through a coffee filter.

As an added bonus, you come out of this with some awesome spiked peach slices! Don't waste them. Believe me, they will be a hit at any party!

Liqueurs

Okay, so the preceding recipe for Peach Schnapps is technically a liqueur, but there are many other liqueurs that you can also make at home. Most liqueurs are made using your already distilled spirits, usually vodka, and flavored. I have only included a few here, as a complete book could be devoted just to home liqueur recipes.

Coffee Liqueur

What coffee lover does not love coffee-flavored liqueur? This is one of the most common liqueurs made at home, and there are countless variations.

Ingredients:

3 cups water

3 cups vodka

2 cups turbinado or raw sugar

½ cup freshly ground dark roast coffee

1 vanilla bean, sliced

Heat water to a boil, remove from heat, and add coffee. Cover and allow to sit for 30 minutes. Return pot to heat and add sugar, stirring until fully dissolved. Add vanilla bean, cover, and allow mixture to cool. Add vodka and pour into quart jars. Seal and allow to rest for 2 weeks. Filter through coffee filter into liquor bottles.

Irish Cream

2 cups Irish or malt whiskey

1½ cups heavy cream

1 can sweetened condensed milk

1 teaspoon instant coffee

2 tablespoons chocolate syrup

1 teaspoon vanilla extract

Combine whiskey, sweetened condensed milk, coffee, chocolate syrup, and vanilla extract in a blender. Blend on highest speed for 30 seconds. Add cream and shake to mix. Pour into sealable glass bottles and refrigerate.

Apple Jack (Apple Pie)

This has become an extremely popular liqueur among home distillers, with variations found on almost every home distilling forum on the Internet. Below is one basic recipe, but feel free to adjust quantities of the ingredients to tailor it to your own tastes.

1.25 quarts apple cider

1.25 quarts apple juice

½ cup sugar

5 cinnamon sticks

1.5 quarts vodka

Heat cider and apple juice in a stock pot. Add sugar and stir until dissolved. Add cinnamon sticks, remove from heat, cover, and allow mixture to sit for approximately an hour. Add vodka and filter through coffee filter into bottles or canning jars. Seal and allow to age for two to four weeks.

8. Drink Recipes

NOW THAT YOU have all of this liquor and liqueur on hand, you need something to make with it. In addition to some of the basic, run-of-the-mill stuff, we have a few unique drinks to try out.

Fuzzy Navel

This old classic seems to have been disappearing. It is a simple drink, but deserves a place here because many people have likely never heard of it or have forgotten about it over time.

3 ounces peach schnapps
3 ounces orange juice

Pour peach schnapps into a highball glass with crushed ice. Top up with orange juice.

For an added twist, you can turn this drink into a Hairy Navel by adding 1 ounce of vodka.

Candy Apple

For those who like a fruity drink that virtually masks the alcohol entirely, this is for you.

1 ounce vodka
3 ounces lemon-lime soda
1½ ounces bar lime mix
½ ounce grenadine

Combine all ingredients in a tall glass with crushed ice. Stir and enjoy!

Creamsicle

1 ounce vanilla vodka

½ ounce triple sec

3 ounces orange juice

1 ounce half-and-half

Combine ingredients in a cocktail shaker with crushed ice. Shake to mix, then pour over ice into a tall glass.

Mudslide

1 ounce vodka

1 ounce coffee liqueur

1 ounce Irish cream liqueur

Combine ingredients in a cock-tail shaker with crushed ice. Shake to mix, then pour over ice.

Sex on the Beach

1½ ounces vodka

1 ounce peach schnapps

1½ ounce cranberry juice

1½ ounces orange juice

1 ounce pineapple juice

Mix all ingredients in a cocktail shaker with ice cubes. Pour over ice into a tall glass and garnish with an orange slice and maraschino cherry.

Long Island Iced Tea

½ ounce triple sec

1 ounce light rum

1 ounce vodka

1 ounce gin

1 ounce tequila

½ teaspoon lemon juice

2 ounce cola

Combine all ingredients except the cola in a cocktail shaker with ice. Shake to blend, then pour into a tall glass and top with cola.

Cherry Bomb

Not a drink, but a great addition to any party. Soak fresh cherries, peach slices, etc., in vodka for at least 24 hours. Pour off vodka and serve!

Jell-O Shots

1 3-ounce package of Jell-O mix, flavor of your choice
1 cup water
1 cup vodka

Pour gelatin mix into a bowl. Bring water to a boil and add to gelatin mix, stirring until fully dissolved. Stir in vodka. Pour into a baking pan and refrigerate until the gelatin has fully set. Cut into cubes and serve.

Nuclear Jell-O Shots

Mix gelatin as noted above, but pour into ice cube trays. To each cube, add one Cherry Bomb. Refrigerate until fully set and serve.

White Russian

2 ounces vodka
1 ounce coffee liqueur
1 ounce half-and-half

Blend all ingredients in a cocktail shaker with ice cubes. Pour over ice into a short glass.

Franklin

Thank you, Franklin, for introducing this simple yet delicious drink to my wife on a trip to Costa Rica. It may have been just you conjuring something up, but it became one of her favorites.

    2 ounces coconut rum
    4 ounces fresh pineapple
    1 tablespoon sugar
    2 ounces crushed ice

Combine all ingredients in a blender and blend on highest speed until smooth. It may be necessary to add more coconut rum to get this to blend properly (darn!).

Mojito

Made well, this is the most refreshing and dangerous drink that I have found. It is danger-ous *because* it is so refreshing, and because a large part of the volume is alcohol—so they can disappear quickly and put you on the floor almost as fast.

    1½ ounces light rum
    1 lime
    8-10 fresh mint leaves
    1 teaspoon sugar
    ½-1 ounce club soda
    ½-1 ounce ginger ale

Cut the peel from the lime and cut into quarters. Put lime

and mint leaves into a sturdy glass and crush using a muddler. Add sugar and muddle again. Fill the glass approximately three-quarters full with crushed ice. Add rum. Top with equal amounts of club soda and ginger ale. Stir to mix.

Tequila Sunrise

2 ounces tequila
4 ounces orange juice
½ ounce grenadine

Add the tequila and orange juice to a tall glass with ice and stir. Tilt the glass and pour a shot of grenadine down the side of the glass so that it goes all the way to the bottom.

Brown Cow

1½ ounce coffee liqueur
4 ounces milk

Combine ingredients in a cocktail shaker with ice. Pour over ice into old-fashioned cocktail glass.

PART (3)

Resources

Frequently Asked Questions

Is hobby distilling legal?

In most countries, no. In some countries you can obtain licensing to distill fuel alcohol. Some states or provinces in your country may allow it, while the federal government does not. In short, do your homework and check with your municipal, state/provincial government, and federal government.

Is distilling difficult?

Distilling is not difficult, but it does require multiple steps, some special equipment, and patience. If you have ever made beer or wine, then you are already halfway there.

How much does it cost to make my own?

That depends on many factors, such as the ingredients you select and how much work you are willing to do to get the necessary sugars used to make alcohol. Generally, the more refined the sugar source (e.g., granulated white sugar from the supermarket vs. feed corn), the higher the cost. Most hobbyists consider quality first for beverage alcohol and cost first for fuel alcohol.

How much distillate will I get?

This is a question that gets asked more times than I can count. What percentage of alcohol was in your wash after fermentation? How much wash are you distilling? Are you distilling in pot mode and getting around 60%abv when everything is combined, or are you distilling in reflux and getting 90 to 95%abv? Despite what people want to hear when they ask this question, there are far too many variables to just spout a number.

How long does it take to distill?

There are far too many things that need to be considered to give even a remote time estimate. The heat source, amount of alcohol in the wash, volume of wash, and distillation method all play a role.

Problems/Solutions

Problem	Possible Cause	Solution
Stuck fermentation	Lack of nutrients for yeast	Add distiller's nutrients
	Wash is too cold	Increase temperature
	Wash got too hot	Yeast has been killed. If specific gravity is high (very little fermentation has taken place), try adding more yeast.
	Too much sugar for strain of yeast	Reduce sugar concentration by adding water.
Fluctuating temperature during reflux	Heat source is cycling	Use a noncycling heat source
	Distilling is being affected by breeze or wind	Protect distiller from wind
	Cooling water temperature or flow rate is changing	Keep temperature of cooling water and rate of flow consistent
Rising temperature at head (reflux)	All alcohol has been collected	Stop collecting and shut down distiller
	Too much heat	Reduce heat input
	Inadequate cooling	Reduce heat, decrease temperature of cooling water, or increase flow of cooling water
Lid lifting (countertop distiller)	Overfilled boiler	Turn distiller off and allow to cool. Remove some liquid to reduce fill level
	Foaming	Turn distiller off and allow to cool. Remove some liquid to reduce fill level. Add anti-foam agent to reduce foaming

Calculations

Calculate %abv in the wash after fermentation has completed:

(Original S.G. - Final S.G.) x 131.25 = %abv

e.g., Original S.G of 1.100, Final S.G. of 0.990

(1.100 - 0.990) x 131.25 = 14.44%abv

Calculate volume of alcohol in wash:

Volume of wash x %abv ÷ 100

e.g., 5 gallons of wash at 14%abv

5 gallons x 14% ÷ 100 = 0.70 gallons

How much water to use for cutting to specific %abv:

(Volume of distillate x %abv of distillate ÷ desired %abv)
    - Volume of distillate

e.g., 1 gallon of distillate @ 90%abv, and you wish to dilute it to
    40%abv

(1 gallon x 90% ÷ 40%) - 1 gallon = 1.25 gallons

How much spirit to use to get X amount of product at a certain %abv:

Desired volume of spirit x desired %abv ÷ original spirit %abv

e.g., You desire 2 gallons @ 40%abv and are starting with spirit
    at 90%abv

2 gallons x 40%abv ÷ 90%abv = 0.89 gallons

Common Setup Methods

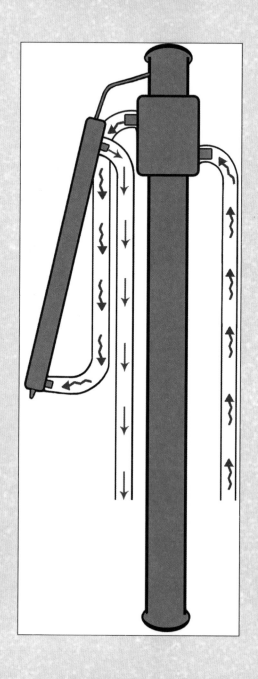

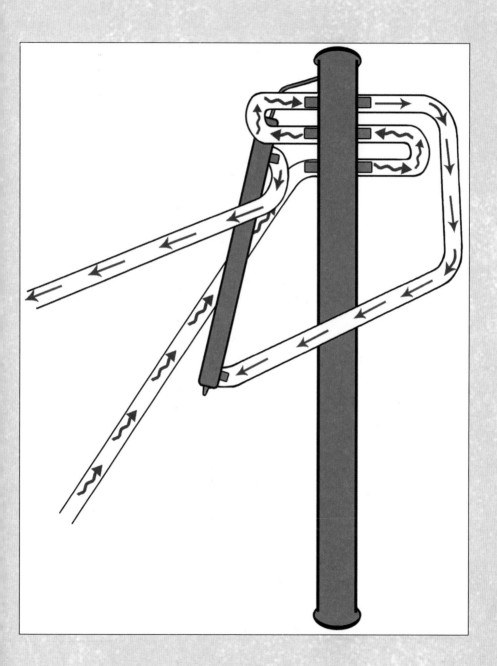

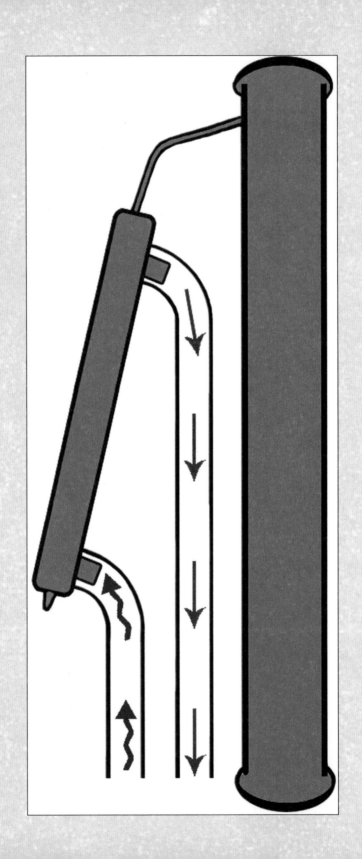

Record-Keeping Log

Batch Log

Batch _____

Date _____

Ingredient   **Weight**

_____   _____

_____   _____

_____   _____

_____   _____

_____   _____

_____   _____

_____   _____

_____   _____

Mixing Instructions _____

_____

_____

_____

Date _____ | Time _____

OG _____

pH _____

Temp _____

Time for ferment to start _____

Date _____ | Time _____

SG _____

pH _____

Temp _____

Comments _____

Date _____ | Time _____

SG _____

pH _____

Temp _____

Comments _____

Date _____ | Time _____

SG _____

pH _____

Temp _____

Comments _____

Date _____ | Time _____

SG _____

pH _____

Temp _____

Comments _____

Glossary

Activated Carbon: (or **activated charcoal**) is used to filter spirits after distillation to remove flavor and aroma. It is produced from many different materials through a combination of carbonization and chemical activation.

Aging: the process of storing distilled spirits in wood barrels—most commonly made of oak—to enhance and alter the flavor. The aging process can last from a few weeks to many years depending on the desired effect.

Airlock: (or **vapor lock**) an inexpensive type of one-way valve that uses water to act as the control. During fermentation, it allows gases formed to escape while blocking outside air that contains oxygen and spoilage organisms.

Alcoholmeter: an instrument used to read the alcohol percentage of a distilled spirit.

Alembic Distiller: one of, if not the oldest true distiller designs almost exclusively made from copper sheet, making them as unique as they are beautiful.

Alpha Amylase: an enzyme that breaks long-chained sugars down by chopping them into smaller bits. It is aggressive, rapidly breaking bonds of starch in the middle and producing random sugars (dextrins). It continues to break these chains down until they become chains of one, two, or three glucose molecules, which can be fermented by the yeast.

Anti-foam Agent: an ingredient used to reduce foaming, either during fermentation or distillation Anti-foam agents work by altering the surface tension of the bubbles that form, causing them to break more quickly than if an anti-foam agent is not used. This reduces the buildup of foam on the surface of the liquid and reduces the issues that can come from foam buildup.

Beta Amylase: an Enzyme that breaks small pieces from the ends of sugar chains. This process is known as saccharification. Beta amylase will preferentially produce two-chained sugars known as maltose.

Carboy: a piece of equipment that is similar in shape to that of a five-gallon plastic water jug, although it is more commonly made of glass. While a carboy is not generally used in spirit production, it is used in winemaking and beer brewing where secondary fermentation is employed.

Clearing Agent: (or **fining**) an agent used once fermentation is complete to speed clearing of the wash, by rapidly settling suspended particles to the bottom of the fermenter.

Congeners: substances other than ethanol alcohol, such as methanol, fusel alcohol, and other alcohols, produced during fermentation, which can contribute positively or negatively to the flavor of the final spirit.

Cooling Water: cold water that is run through the still to force reflux action or to condense the alcohol vapor that is drawn from the still.

Distilling: is simply a means of purifying a liquid by boiling the liquid and then condensing the vapor. Therefore, if the product that you wish to collect is not present in the liquid that you are distilling, it will not be present after distillation.

Equipment Cleaner: specially designed chemicals that remove some of the organic and inorganic buildup on the equipment that you cannot see. It is used in addition to regular soap and water.

Equipment Sanitizer: chemicals used to remove spoilage organisms from your fermentation and distillation equipment which could otherwise contaminate you wash, such as household bleach, alcohol, Star San, and CTSP, just to name a few. However, do not confuse sanitizing with sterilization, which is not necessary.

Ethanol: the specific kind of alcohol being referred to when the term alcohol is used in regards to distilling. While there are many other kinds of alcohol, ethanol is what we want to consume in an alcoholic beverage.

External Valved Reflux: an extremely popular still design that is widely used by people building their own columns. As the name suggests, the forcing of reflux takes place outside of the main column body. The column rises from the boiler with either a 90-degree elbow, or more commonly a tee fitting, at the top of the column.

Fermenter: (or **Primary**) a food grade container used to mix ingredients and hold the wash during the fermentation process.

Fermentation: the process where yeast consumes sugar and converts it into alcohol.

Flavoring: the intentional addition of specific flavors, such as fruit or natural extracts, not the flavors that are contributed by aging in an oak barrel.

Forced Reflux Still: a column still that has the addition of some form of vapor cooling to help improve efficiency and effectiveness to ensure that maximum distillate purity is achieved.

Foreshots: the first parts of the wash to come off during the distillation process. They consist of methanol and other volatiles, such as acetone and aldehydes, which should be separated from the rest of the distillate and discarded.

Gluco Amylase: (or **Gamma Amylase** or **Amyloglucosidase**) an Enzyme that breaks the long pieces of sugar chains from the end of the chains. The advantage to gluco amylase is that it will preferentially create single-chained molecules of glucose, which are highly fermentable by the yeast.

Heads: They are made up primarily of ethanol, but still contain some congeners. They are usually 80%+ abv. It is a good idea to collect the heads separately from the next stage, as you can combine them based on your own tastes.

Hydrometer: a hydrometer is used to find the specific gravity, or density, of your wash compared to that of pure water.

Infusion: a method used to add flavor to your spirits during the distillation process by suspending material in the vapor path and allowing the alcohol vapors extract flavor and aroma compounds.

Internal Valved Reflux: a variation of the external valved reflux still where the forcing of reflux is brought inside the column. The result is a better, sleeker appearance, but this does not substantially alter the performance or basic operation of the column.

Krausen: a layer of foam that forms on top of the wash during the aerobic respiration phase. How large the Krausen is will depend on your strain of yeast and the composition of your wash.

Lag Phase: the period in which the yeast is multiplying in the wash. Generally, you will see little visible action during this phase, aside from a slight head of yeast building on the top of your wash. It can range from less than an hour to as much as a day.

Making Cuts: the point at which you start and stop collecting the distillate in order to collect specific components.

Maximum Alcohol Tolerance: the percentage of alcohol that yeast can build its tolerance to. As yeast converts more and more sugar into alcohol and the percentage of alcohol in the wash rises, so does the yeast's tolerance to alcohol.

Middle Run: the bulk of the distillate that you will be keeping as drinking alcohol. It will have fewer congeners and be less harsh than the heads, and will start at around 80%abv, dropping down to around 60-65%abv.

Parrot: a tool connected between the condenser and collection container so that the distillate flows through it on its way to your container. The parrot holds your alcoholmeter, allowing you to take real-time readings of the alcohol percentage as the distillate is being produced.

Polishing: (or **filtering**) a process in which you remove congeners remaining in the spirits even after distillation. It is used almost exclusively in the production of neutral spirits (vodka) and is most commonly done by running the distilled spirits through activated carbon.

Pot Distilling: the more traditional method of distillation that is generally used for making spirits such as whiskey, brandy and other flavored spirits.

Racking: the process of transferring the wash from one container to another, such as from a primary fermenter into a carboy or kettle, using a siphon.

Reflux Distilling: the process of distilling using a tall distillation column to facilitate greater separation of the components in the wash, which allows more control over the composition of the final spirit. Reflux distilling has the ability to produce a highly refined, very pure distillate.

Sedimentation: the settling of yeast and suspended particles to the bottom of the fermenter.

Siphon: A siphon is used to transfer, or "rack," liquid from one container to another. A homebrew-style siphon will have a rigid cane-shaped piece of tube (known as a racking cane) that can be placed in your fermenter, ensuring that you reach the bottom of the vessel.

On the bottom of the racking cane there should be a plastic tip, known as an anti-sediment tip. The purpose of the anti-sediment tip is to reduce the amount of sediment in the fermenter from being carried over during racking.

Sugar Wash: a simple wash that is a combination of sugar and water. However, since a sugar wash provides no nutrition for yeast, you must either add a complete nutrient complex or use turbo yeast.

Tails: the last part of the wash to come off during the distillation process that are of any value (over 203°F (95°C)). Tails contain the last bit of ethanol and are usually added to the kettle along with the next wash in order to recover the ethanol.

Test Cylinder: a tall, narrow cylinder that is used to hold a sample of liquid for testing with your hydrometer or alcoholmeter. They can be made of either glass or plastic, but if you intend to use the cylinder for testing your distilled spirits, then you must use either glass or chemical-tolerant plastic.

The "Hillbilly" Still: the backwoods version of a pot distiller that is meant for large production, not premium quality. This type of distiller often has a kettle ranging in size from 50 gallons to several hundreds of gallons, and it is frequently heated over an open wood fire. They will sometimes have a thermometer built in, but more often than not no mind is paid to the temperature in the backwoods. The hillbilly type of still works much the same as an alembic still and is intended solely for pot distillation. To condense the larger amount of distillate being produced, this type of still uses a long coil of copper, known as a worm, to condense vapor using the surrounding air as a form of heat exchanger.

Thumper Still: (or "doubler" or "thump keg") an added piece of equipment between the kettle and the condenser. It is used as an economical method of achieving similar results to the process of double distilling.

Wash: a liquid mixture that contains yeast and sugar for the purpose of creating alcohol through fermentation that can then be distilled.

Yeast: properly defined as a fungus, it is a single-celled organism that consumes sugar in an aqueous solution and converts it into alcohol.

Index